PROVERBS & PARABLES

PARABLE OF THE LOST SHEEP ~ A CONVERSATION BETWEEN A PHARISEE AND JESUS ...

New Creation Publications

Ralph Ellis Miley
Publisher and Project Organizer

Don Ensign
Art Director and Editor

Kevin Yong
Editor

George Macas, Jr.
Marketing Consultant

Nate Butler
Alec Stevens
Consultants

PROVERBS AND PARABLES
Published by New Creation Publications, P.O. Box 254, Temple City, CA 91780
in association with the Christian Comic Arts Society (CCAS). Covers and compilation copyright
©1998 New Creation Publications, All Rights Reserved. No part of this book may be used or
reproduced in any manner without written permission of the individual copyright owners
except in the context of reviews.

Printed in the U.S.A.
First Printing

ISBN 0-9665118-0-8
Library of Congress Catalog Card Number: 98-66069
Individual Trademarks and Copyrights on page iii

Cover Art:
Pencils.........Gary Shipman
Inks..............Danny Bulanadi
Colors...........Steve Firchow
Graphics.......Clint Johnson
Collage........Ralph Miley
Layout:........Hal Jones

Principal Letterers: Don and Laura Chin, Don Ensign

TABLE OF CONTENTS

PARABLES

Cartoons, creativity and Christ!

What a tremendous combination for communicating.

Comics are a graphic medium and in an age of busy lives that allow little time for reading, pictures seem to get priority. TV demands attention and then mesmerizes. Comics present just as much action and because of their compact, streamlined format they truly entertain.

Those of us who have been involved in creating Christian comics realize that the average reader wants to be entertained. They buy a comic for fun and excitement. And we provide that— but it's only a book.

We want the reader to pick up our books, be anxious to turn the page and to become totally involved in the story line.

So, yes, our job is to entertain, but our goal is to offer something far more important than slapstick and suspense. Folks by the thousands are seeking all kinds of thrills and kicks to escape the reality of life. Our great motivation is to take a slice of life that the reader can identify with, and then show precisely how God wants to be involved in that life experience. In short, to illustrate in a very practical way the tremendous difference that having a personal relationship with Jesus Christ can have, day in and day out in the very nitty-gritty of our lives.

Jesus wants us to enjoy the wonder of life's adventure, and to enjoy it abundantly, positively and fruitfully. All of us involved in Christian comics are thankful to God for the talent He gave us.

It's a privilege to give it back to Him. He is our creator. Through Him we draw and have our being.

Al Hartley

On the Making of Proverbs and Parables

It has been said that the way to tell a story is to start at the beginning, keep going until you reach the end, and then stop. It sounds easy enough. Finding the beginning, that's the hard part. When asked to explain the origins of a project like this, where do I begin? At the time it was first proposed? How about the ideas that led up to the proposal? How about the events that led up to the ideas? However, as hard as it is to pinpoint the true beginning, every story has to start somewhere. The big comic book convention in San Diego is as good a place as any.

It was 1996, and a few Christian comic enthusiasts had decided to meet at the newly renamed Comic-Con International: San Diego. Merely by word-of-mouth invitation, that small informal gathering grew into a meeting of dozens of Christian comic fans, small-pressers, and professionals.

"I thought I was the only one!" was the motto of the meeting, and everyone involved sensed that the Christian comics movement was about to start picking up momentum. Within a year, we would be seeing not only informal meetings, but also tables, panel discussions, and even chapel services at various comic conventions across the nation.

Once the lonely Christians involved in the comics industry had found each other, then what? The *Alpha-Omega* apazine existed for the amateurs, the *New Creation* newsletter served as a lifeline for the fans, but what could be done for the professionals?

Many involved in the industry talked wistfully of collaborating on a "Christian comics" project, of using their artistic talents not just to entertain but also to make a statement for their faith. Unfortunately, although the desire was there, the opportunity seemed out of reach. Everyone's schedules were already quite busy just working on projects to pay the bills. Few had time for any outside work of more than two or three pages. Things seemed hopeless, until someone finally asked:

"So... how about a project where we each contribute only two or three pages?"

As blatantly obvious as such a solution sounds, it takes time to work out the details. *New Creation's* Executive Editor, Ralph Ellis Miley, had been working since 1994 on an idea for a comic book featuring short adaptations of scripture. (His artwork included in this anthology is a holdover from that earlier project.) The idea languished until Ralph was asked to review Paradox Press' *Big Book Of Martyrs*, a massive trade paperback anthology which featured short, self-contained stories built around a common theme. Inspired and encouraged that such a book *was* actually possible, Ralph spearheaded the new project that would eventually become *Proverbs and Parables*.

Instead of a comic book, we were now hoping for a trade paperback. Instead of a "shotgun" anthology of various topics, we now worked to ensure a focused theme. Specifically, we wanted it to be Biblical in nature (as that was what brought us all together in the first place) but not merely a comic adaptation of familiar Bible stories. Not only had such adaptations been done many times before, but whatever scriptures we planned to work with needed to be short, pithy, to-the-point, and easily lend themselves to visual storytelling. The parables of Jesus were perfectly suited, as were the proverbs of the Old Testament.

At first, we thought to make an anthology simply of modern retellings of the parables. One such example of this was submitted by veteran comic artist Jay Disbrow. (See following pages.)

Jay's art was great, as was his modern adaptation of the parable. However, as the number of artists continued to grow, we realized that so many full retellings could easily make the book seem jumbled and unfocused. We needed a common theme, a unifying stylistic element that could tie these vastly different art styles and genres together.

Ultimately, we decided upon a guideline allowing for any kind of visual adaptation as long as the only text accompanying it were the actual Bible verses. No new dialogue, no extra narration, just pure scripture. Of course, this required that all artists start with a common translation of the Bible for their text. The classic King James Version eventu-

The UNCARING Magistrate

ADAPTED AND ILLUSTRATED BY *Jay Disbrow*

OUR LORD TOLD HIS DISCIPLES THE PARABLE OF THE JUDGE WHO WAS INDIFFERENT TO HIS DUTIES AS A DEFENDER OF THE PEOPLE. THIS STORY IS AN EXAMPLE OF THE ETERNAL TRUTH THAT SOCIETY MUST BE GOVERNED BY GODLY WISDOM, OR RULED BY TYRANNICAL DESPOTISM.

LUKE 18:1-8

WE FIND THAT THE CASE OF MARY HOWELWORTH VS. CONWAY REALITY IS LACKING IN CREDIBLE EVIDENCE. THE CASE IS DISMISSED!

NO! NO, YOUR HONOR! THEY TOOK MY LIFE SAVINGS! THEY MUST PAY IT BACK!

CONGRATULATIONS MR. CONWAY. YOU HAVE ONCE AGAIN PROVED YOUR INNOCENCE IN A COURT OF LAW.

OF COURSE. I ALWAYS HAD FAITH IN OUR JUDICIAL SYSTEM. AND HAVING THE BEST OF LAWYERS DIDN'T HURT EITHER!

YOUR HONOR PLEASE, YOU MUST HELP ME GET MY MONEY BACK. I HAVE NOTHING TO LIVE ON! THEY TOOK EVERYTHING!

HOW DID YOU GET INTO MY PRIVATE CHAMBERS?-- I CAN DO NOTHING FOR YOU, WIDOW HOWELWORTH. YOU FAILED TO PRODUCE PROOF OF YOUR CLAIMS.

BUT THEY TOOK MY MONEY AND GAVE ME NOTHING IN RETURN! YOU SAW THE CANCELED CHECKS I SENT THEM.

BUT THEY DO *NOT* PROVE INTENT TO DEFRAUD. IF YOU WANT TO WIN YOUR CASE, HIRE A GOOD LAWYER.

BUT I HAVE NO MONEY LEFT FOR A LAWYER! THEY TOOK IT ALL! OH GOD, WHAT CAN I DO?

PERHAPS GOD WILL HELP YOU, BUT I DOUBT IT. I HAVE NO FAITH IN EITHER GOD NOR MAN!

TWO NIGHTS LATER, THE WIFE OF THE JUDGE APPROACHED HIM.

THAT WIDOW CAME TO YOU AGAIN TODAY, DIDN'T SHE, HAROLD?

YES, SHE WAS NAGGING ME FOR A HALF HOUR! I HAD TO GET THE BAILIFF TO TAKE HER OUT!

WELL, I THINK SHE'S RIGHT! YOU SHOULD DO SOMETHING TO HELP HER!

WHAT CAN I DO? I HAVE TO WORK WITHIN THE CONFINES OF THE LAW! I CAN'T JUST MAKE RULINGS BASED ON EMOTIONS!

THE NEXT DAY, ON THE GOLF LINKS--

PLEASE, YOUR HONOR, YOU MUST HELP ME GET JUSTICE. I CAN'T GO ON LIKE THIS!

YOU AGAIN! I CAN'T EVEN ENJOY A ROUND OF GOLF WITHOUT YOU SHOWING UP!

BUT I'M GOING TO BE EVICTED FROM MY HOME! I DON'T HAVE THE MONEY TO PAY MY PROPERTY TAXES! YOU'RE THE ONLY ONE WHO CAN HELP ME!

THAT'S NOT MY CONCERN, MRS. HOWELWORTH. ONE OF YOUR CHILDREN WILL HAVE TO TAKE YOU IN!---- NOW PLEASE STAND ASIDE.

LATER THAT DAY--

THAT WOMAN IS DRIVING ME INSANE WITH HER CONSTANT ENTREATIES! EVEN THOUGH I DON'T FEAR GOD, OR RESPECT MAN, I'LL HAVE TO DO RIGHT BY HER, OR SHE'LL WEAR ME OUT BY HER CONSTANT NAGGING!

THE NEXT DAY--

YOU WANT ME TO INVESTIGATE CONWAY REALITY, JUDGE? IS THIS RELATED TO THE HOWELWORTH CASE?

YES! EVERYONE SUSPECTS THAT CONWAY IS A CROOK! I'VE GOT TO PROVE IT, AND GET THAT WOMAN'S MONEY BACK OR SHE WILL DRIVE ME BATTY!

THREE MONTHS LATER—

AUGUSTUS CONWAY, YOU HAVE BEEN FOUND GUILTY OF FRAUD AND CRIMINAL EMBEZZLEMENT! YOU WILL RETURN TO MRS. HOWELWORTH HER FULL CASH INVESTMENT, PLUS 25% INTEREST, AND YOU WILL SERVE THREE YEARS IN THE STATE PENITENTIARY!

AND OUR LORD CONCLUDED HIS STORY BY SAYING-- HEAR WHAT THE UNJUST JUDGE SAYS. AND WILL NOT GOD BRING JUSTICE FOR HIS CHOSEN ONES WHO CRY OUT TO HIM DAY AND NIGHT? WILL HE KEEP PUTTING THEM OFF? I TELL YOU HE WILL SEE THAT THEY GET JUSTICE, AND QUICKLY.

THE END

ally won out. Some variations from the rules (and minor changes to the text) have since crept in, but at least it gave us a framework to build upon. *Proverbs and Parables* was underway.

This book was originally intended as a project for the members of *Alpha-Omega*. However, the number of participants rapidly grew as friends-of-friends began passing the word among their fellow Christian artists. The ranks of seasoned professionals, dedicated amateurs and eager first-timers soon became so large that we were running out of proverbs and parables to assign. It was a problem that we didn't mind in the least.

Many delays and unanticipated problems still lay ahead, but God has seen our humble efforts through to completion.

May our imaginations be kindled by these *Proverbs and Parables*, by these words of the wise and the wisdom of Jesus, the Living Word.

"GIVING THANKS" BY RALPH ELLIS MILEY

In an age where all of us are striving to get through the business of day to day living, there should be a time to pause and give thanks for our many blessings. Whether it be for our job, health, family, friends, or just another day of life, we should give thanks. On the television, we see athletes and entertainers give thanks to the people who have contributed in some way towards the receiving of an award in their given field. Some of these athletes and entertainers who are honored give thanks to God. They recognize the fact that the Lord has not only allowed them to be involved in their desired profession, but He has allowed them some measure of success. This is part of His divine plan for their lives.

All of us have a destiny to fulfill as we go about the business of day to day living. Some of us dream about it for years, but dreaming alone does not help us reach that goal. Some of us press towards that goal for years, but unfortunately with the passage of time we lose hope and give up, never to see that dream become a reality.

As we strive to fulfill our destiny, there can be an event that causes us to realize we're witnessing a sovereign move of God. He gives us hope and we are privileged and humbled that the One who orchestrates the movements of the universe allows us to be a part of the fulfillment of His plan for our lives. It is a time to pause and give thanks to Him.

This *Proverbs and Parables* project humbles me and causes me to give thanks to the Lord. For it was the Lord who brought together over sixty Christian artists from different denominations, races, backgrounds, and countries to work together on one project. Professionals, aspiring professionals, and amateurs have given of their time and talent to honor God with their art. It puts me in awe of God's greatness, mercy, and grace. Thanks must go to each and every artist who contributed to this book. Many, if not all, of them prayed and sought the Lord as to their contribution to this united effort. Special thanks goes to Nate Butler and Alec Stevens, who put us in contact with many of the artists in this book. To the artists who pulled double and triple duty; Jesse Hamm, Danny Bulanadi, Clint Johnson, and Michael James. To those who contributed financially to this project; Benjamin J. Schmitz, Shadow McKenna, James E. Miller, and Pauline Miley. To Don and Laura Chin at Express Press for their outstanding lettering and production work. To Harold Buchholz, for arranging the printing and for producing an excellent package. To veteran Christian artist Al Hartley, for graciously writing the foreword. To editor Kevin Yong, for the many hours going through Scriptures, assigning these Scriptures to different artists, editing, assisting in typesetting, page layout and support for this project. To art director and editor Don Ensign (father of Christian comic fandom) for long hours involved in page layout, typesetting, editing, and support. For my wife, Desiree Miley, for putting up with my obsession for this project and also seeing God's hand in it. And to all those who prayed that this project would honor God and minister to the readers.

My apologies to those artists whose work I was not able to include. I hope we will still be able to work together on other projects in the future, Lord willing.

And finally, "In everything give thanks, for this is the will of God in Christ Jesus concerning you." I Thessalonians 5:18.

A Very Short and Personal History of Christian Comics

According to art historian Harry W. Miller, comics in general and Christian comics in particular had their roots in early books like the Joshua Rotolus (5th-6th century AD), the Utrecht Psalmer (830 AD), and the German colored woodcut of the Horsemen of the Apocalypse (ca. 1465). Each of these has sequences of pictures with words—the heart of what modern comics are. Be that as it may, our history of Christian comic books starts much later in time.

The Christian comic book genre is itself divided into several sub-categories. These sub-categories are the Bible adaptation comics, the Christian adventure comics and more recently several subdivisions within the contemporary Christian comic book movement that is largely centered, though not exclusively, around the direct sales market.

One of the fathers of the American comic book and of the first superhero, Superman, was also the first to develop the Bible comic. MC Gaines published the first issues of *Picture Stories from the Bible* in 1942. These adaptations were written by Sunday school teacher Montgomery Mulford and drawn by Don Cameron. Another entry into this genre was religious publisher David C. Cook's *The Picture Bible*. This rather extensive adaptation of the Old and New Testament was

THEN DAVID RUNS UP TO GOLIATH, AND WITH GOLIATH'S OWN SWORD CUTS OFF HIS HEAD ~

scripted by Iva Hoth and superbly drawn by one of Will Eisner's early associates, Andre LeBlanc. This first appeared in serialized form in the Sunday school handout, *Sunday Pixs* during the 1950s and 60s and was later collected in book editions (1973, 1978). More recent noteworthy efforts have been DC Comics' *The Bible* (1975), written by Sheldon Mayer and illustrated by Nestor Redondo. The United Bible Society produced a series of gorgeously painted comics (such as *The Great Fisherman*, 1983). In the 1980s, Tyndale House Publishers came out with a series of "Cosmics" that were humorous adaptations of Bible stories like *Moses The Man Who Talked To Bushes* (1987) by cartoonist Win Mumma. Most recently independent publisher Leo Bak produced the very liter-

al and dramatic depiction of the last book of the Bible called *Revelation: The Comic Book*. (1995)

Perhaps bridging the gap between direct Bible comic adaptations and adventure comics was "Tullus", written by Joseph Hughes Newton for David C. Cook. This historical fiction period piece took place in New Testament times and follows the adventures of a teenaged Christian. These stories began in late 1943 and appeared in Sunday School take-home papers similar to the aforementioned *Picture Bible*.

One of the most memorable individuals to enter this arena in the 1960s was Jack T. Chick. Chick started out publishing small black and white comic book tracts such as *Holy Joe*, which presented the Christian gospel in very stark, unapologetic terms. Over the years Chick also produced a series of full-sized color comics called the "Crusader Series." In this series, the heroes have adventures smuggling Bibles behind the Iron Curtain (*Operation Bucharest*, 1974), struggling against demon possession (*Exorcists* 1975) and battling bigoted evolutionists (*Primal Man*, 1976). The later issues became highly controversial as Chick began waging a vigorous literary war against the Jesuits in particular and the Roman Catholic church in general.

In the early 1970s the Fleming H. Revell Company began their Spire Christian Comics line with such titles as *David Wilkerson's The Cross and the Switchblade* (1972) and Brother Andrew's *God's Smuggler* (1972). These stories were well drawn by comic book veteran Al Hartley. Later on, Spire also licensed the rights to use Archie, Jughead, Betty and Veronica from the Archie Comics Group to produce a rather odd hybrid commonly known as the "Archie Christian Comics." Hartley also produced the art on these comics. Perhaps an even stranger association was the abortive relationship between Thomas Nelson and Marvel Comics. In the early 1990s, these two publishing giants produced three issues of a Christian super-hero of sorts called the *Illuminator* (1993), several Bible adaptation comics including *The Life of Christ* (1993) and a "Christian Classics Series" doing updated adaptations of books like John Bunyan's *Pilgrim Progress* (1992).

I have had a ringside seat to observe and take part in the emerging Christian comics movement of the last two decades. My personal involvement in Christian comics began in the early 1960s as a young teenager having just discovered the early flowering of the silver age of comics. One of my early superhero creations was "Dynamic Man" who was a Bible-believing missionary in Central America. In 1964, I developed another Christian superhero called "The Protector" who actually saw print in a fanzine of the time. In 1977, after several years of work, I self-published a comic book called *Tales of Antediluvia* and gave it away at that year's San Diego Comic Convention. This comic even had an abbreviated and authorized version of the Four Spiritual Laws (I was on Campus Crusade for Christ staff then). The observable results from that evangelistic venture were less than impressive. Sometime later, a friend suggested finding other Christians interested in comics books. In May 1984, I published a newsletter called *Valiant* aimed at fellow believers with a love of the comic book medium. *Valiant* lasted 2 1/2 years and ended with a mailing list of 200 people. In March 1985, I launched the amateur press association *Alpha-Omega,* which has served as a Christian communication forum and network on comic book related projects. *Alpha-Omega* is still being published and has produced over 80 issues. Through *Valiant* and *Alpha-Omega* many individuals important to the movement emerged. People like Harry W. Miller, former college art professor; Billy Leavell, ordained minister to the deaf; John G. Pierce, teacher, comics historian and writer; Ralph E. Miley, Los Angeles school teacher; Steven Shipley, former minister and small press publisher (who published *Warrior,* a newsletter similar to *Valiant*); G. Raymond Eddy, creator of the delightful angel mouse, Galen the Saintly; and Canadian Bob Wierdsma (publisher of the *Christian Cartoonist & Illustrator*) just to name a few. Various publishing collaborations spun off of *Alpha-Omega* as networking developed between like-minded individuals. People such as Detroit-based Freazie White, Jr teamed up with Alabama artist Mark Poe to produce *Project: New Man* (1991) and *Humants* (1991). Ralph Miley, Jack I. Martin, Charles Whitley and myself produced several issues of *Valiant Efforts* (1988-91) for the direct sales market. I would team up with Ralph Miley and Kevin Yong in 1996 to produce the newsletter *New Creation,* which reports on this burgeon-

ing movement.

One of the most influential Christian comics creators to emerge from this time is Nate Butler. Butler, a working comics professional with credits ranging from Archie to Marvel, produced *Aida-Zee* #1 (1990). Butler rounded up an impressive group of well known comics professionals who professed varying degrees of Christian faith. Kerry Gammill (Superman penciler), Gary Martin (*Nexus* inker), Steve Lightle (*Doom Patrol* penciler), Dick Ayers (Silver age Marvel inker and penciler), Murphy Anderson (DC inker and penciler), and Gaylord Dubois (prolific scripter for Dell and Gold Key comics) were among many who contributed to Butler's tightly managed and edited comic. Butler would go on to team up with Ron Vozar, a Christian games manufacturer, to publish two issues of *Christian Comics & Games Magazine* (1995, 1996). Butler also produced *Parodee* (1993, published by Don Chin) and *Behold 3-D* (1996, published by The Edge Group).

By the late 1980s and early 1990s there was a virtual avalanche of Christian comics creators entering the market. A number of well-defined (and not so well-defined) sub-categories started to appear in the emerging Christian comics movement.

Christian superheroes were represented by the aforementioned work of White, Poe and the *Valiant Efforts* crew. Other entries were professional animator John Celestri with his *The Christian Crusader* (1991) that did well for a time in the Christian book store market. Former *Robotech* artist Reggie Byers published several issues of the *Kidz of the King* (1994). Peter J. King came out with his *Soldier of God* (1997) and Todd Tennant drew the massively rendered *Private Sector* (1995).

About this time, Frank Peretti's novel *This Present Darkness* was making a significant impact on the Christian reading public. Out of this trend came spiritual warfare comics. Eternal Studios of Houston, Texas produced a well-drawn,

computer colored series called *Archangels: The Saga* (1995) which became the best selling Christian comic of the period. Hal Jones of Battleline Comics came out with his very personal *Beyond Human* #1 (1995) and a talented young Matt Martin wrote and drew *Vortex* (1993), a sort of Christianized version of Spawn. James Pruett, managing editor of Caliber Comics, created and wrote the excellent *The Apparition* (1996) series. Angels and demons fought each other in Best Comics' *Battleground Earth* (1997?) by Paul Melletter

and Chuck Angell.

A fantasy sub-genre was represented by *Pakkins Land* (1996), a delightfully tasteful Narnia-like fable by Gary and Rhoda Shipman, and Monte Wilson's *elfin Romance* (1994). The approaching turn of the millennium has produced apocalyptic comics such as Christine Kerrick's superb *Empire* (1997), Eric Jansen's *Freedom Fighter* (1997), and Adam Steadman's *The Antipicator* (1997). There were Christian funny animal comics like *Apathy Kat* by Harold Buchholz (1995), and *Galen The Saintly* by G. Raymond Eddy (1997); Christian ninja comics like Mike S. Miller's

Immortal Two (1997-1998); Christian monster comics like *Monster Mayhem* (1998) by Rick Newby; Christian satire comics such as Jesse Hamm's "Comics To Bore and Confuse You" (1995) from *Scattered* and others.

In summary, Christian comics have served a variety of purposes. The Bible comics were produced to educate less word-oriented generations of children and adults about the wonders of the good book. Publications like Jack Chick's tracts, and comic books like *Aida-Zee,* are straight evangelistic vehicles produced to see people won to faith in Christ. Many of the more recent Christian comics are more entertainment directed. While they are not aimed only at Christians they are at best "pre-evangelistic" to the non-Christian reader. The message is more subtle than up-front. It should be stressed that many of these comics are not all equal in terms of art/story quality or spiritual/theological maturity. Some are very well done while others are diamonds in the rough. But they are all made with much enthusiasm and (hopefully) dedication to the Lord. How much of this work is gold, silver, and precious stones and how much is wood, hay or stubble is for the one righteous God to judge on the last day (I Cor. 3:12-17).

Into this mix the ***Proverbs and Parables*** collection arrives with its vast array of talented Christian artists. We hope that you are blessed, encouraged and edified by this picturization of God's eternal written word.

(This is not meant to be a comprehensive survey of Christian comic books, past or present. If you have been left out of this brief rundown please accept my apologies. Your heavenly reward is far more important than fleeting temporal recognition.)

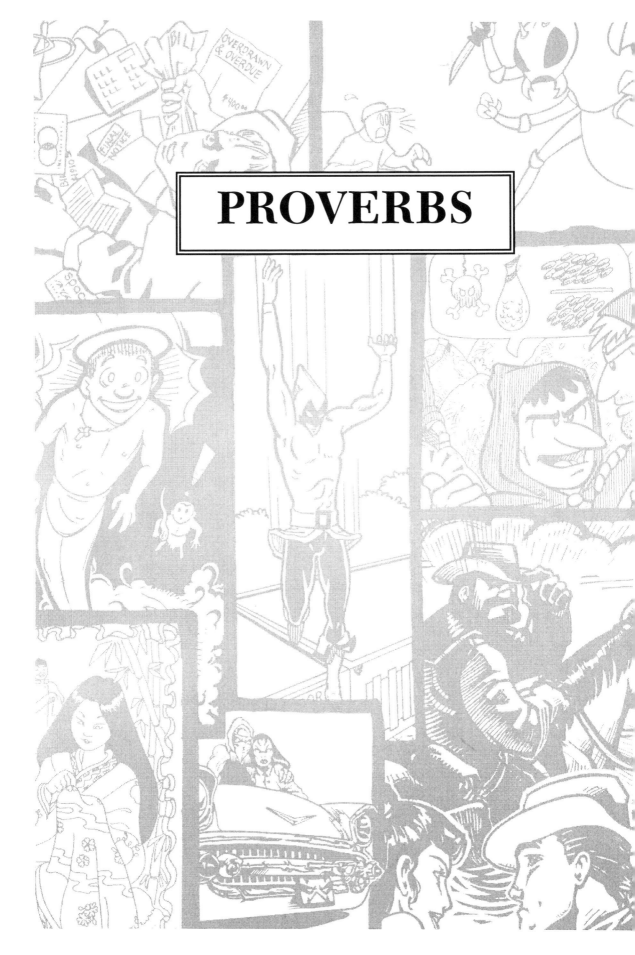

PROVERBS

FORSAKE HER NOT, FOR SHE SHALL PRESERVE THEE: LOVE HER, AND SHE SHALL KEEP THEE. WISDOM IS THE PRINCIPAL THING; THEREFORE GET WISDOM: AND WITH ALL THY GETTING GET UNDERSTANDING. EXALT HER, AND SHE SHALL PROMOTE THEE: SHE SHALL BRING THEE HONOR, WHEN THOU EMBRACE HER.

SHE SHALL GIVE TO THINE HEAD AN ORNAMENT OF GRACE: A CROWN OF GLORY SHALL SHE DELIVER TO THEE.

HEAR YE CHILDREN, THE INSTRUCTION OF A FATHER, AND ATTEND TO KNOW UNDERSTANDING. FOR I WILL GIVE YOU GOOD DOCTRINE, FORSAKE YE NOT MY LAW. FOR I WAS MY FATHER'S SON, TENDER AND ONLY BELOVED IN THE SIGHT OF MY MOTHER. HE TAUGHT ME ALSO, AND SAID UNTO ME, LET THINE HEART RETAIN MY WORDS: KEEP MY COMMANDMENTS, AND LIVE.

HEAR, O MY SON, AND RECEIVE MY SAYINGS; AND THE YEARS OF THY LIFE SHALL BE MANY. I HAVE TAUGHT THEE IN THE WAY OF WISDOM; I HAVE LED THEE IN THE RIGHT PATHS.

THE FEAR OF THE LORD IS TO HATE EVIL: PRIDE, AND ARROGANCY, AND THE EVIL WAY, AND THE FROWARD MOUTH, DO I HATE. COUNSEL IS MINE, AND SOUND WISDOM: I AM UNDERSTANDING; I HAVE STRENGTH. BY ME KINGS REIGN, AND PRINCES DECREE JUSTICE. BY ME PRINCES RULE, AND NOBLES, EVEN ALL THE JUDGES OF THE EARTH. I LOVE THEM THAT LOVE ME; AND THOSE THAT SEEK ME EARLY SHALL FIND ME.

2

PENCILS BY REBECCA BAERMAN
INKS BY JESSE HAMM

MY SON...

IF SINNERS ENTICE YOU, DO NOT CONSENT. IF THEY SAY, COME WITH US...

LET US LAY IN WAIT FOR BLOOD, LET US LURK SECRETLY FOR THE INNOCENT WITHOUT CAUSE.

LET US SWALLOW THEM UP ALIVE AS THE GRAVE; AND WHOLE, AS THOSE THAT GO DOWN INTO THE PIT.

WE SHALL FIND PRECIOUS SUBSTANCE...

WE SHALL FILL OUR HOUSES WITH PLUNDER.

3

CAST IN YOUR LOT AMONG US; LET US ALL HAVE ONE PURSE.

MY SON, DO NOT WALK WITH THEM...

FOR THEIR FEET RUN TO EVIL, AND MAKE HASTE TO SHED BLOOD.

AND THEY LAY IN WAIT FOR THEIR OWN BLOOD, THEY LURK SECRETLY FOR THEIR OWN LIVES.

SO ARE THE WAYS OF EVERY ONE THAT IS GREEDY OF GAIN; WHICH TAKES AWAY THE LIFE OF THE OWNERS.

4

PROVERBS 1:10-19

MY SON, ATTEND UNTO MY WISDOM AND INCLINE YOUR EAR TO MY UNDERSTANDING.

THAT YOU MAY REGARD DISCRETION, AND THAT YOUR LIPS MAY KEEP KNOWLEDGE.

FOR THE LIPS OF A STRANGE WOMAN DRIP HONEY, AND HER MOUTH IS SMOOTHER THAN OIL;

BUT HER END IS BITTER AS WORMWOOD, SHARP AS A TWO-EDGED SWORD.

HER FEET GO DOWN TO DEATH; HER STEPS TAKE HOLD OF HELL. SHE DOES NOT PONDER THE PATH OF LIFE, HER WAYS ARE UNSTABLE AND YOU DO NOT KNOW THEM.

5

ART BY CHRISTINE KERRICK

PROVERBS 5:1-6, 8-11, 18-19

Proverbs 6:16-19

A PROUD LOOK,

A LYING TONGUE,

AND HANDS THAT SHED INNOCENT BLOOD,

A HEART THAT DEVISES WICKED PLANS,

FEET THAT MAKE HASTE TO RUN TO EVIL,

A FALSE WITNESS THAT BREATHES OUT LIES,

AND A MAN WHO SOWS DISCORD AMONG BROTHERS.

ART BY DON A. KELLY

CAN A MAN TAKE FIRE IN HIS BOSOM, AND HIS CLOTHES NOT BE BURNED?

CAN ONE GO UPON HOT COALS, AND HIS FEET NOT BE BURNED?

SO HE THAT GOETH IN TO HIS NEIGHBOR'S WIFE; WHOSOEVER TOUCHETH HER SHALL NOT BE INNOCENT.

ART BY TIM GAGNON

MEN DO NOT DESPISE A THIEF, IF HE STEALS TO SATISFY HIS SOUL WHEN HE IS HUNGRY;

BUT IF HE IS FOUND, HE SHALL RESTORE SEVENFOLD; HE SHALL GIVE ALL THE SUBSTANCE OF HIS HOUSE.

BUT WHOSO COMMITTETH ADULTERY WITH A WOMAN LACKETH UNDERSTANDING: HE THAT DOETH IT DESTROYETH HIS OWN SOUL.

A WOUND AND DISHONOR SHALL HE GET; AND HIS REPROACH SHALL NOT BE WIPED AWAY. FOR JEALOUSY IS THE RAGE OF A MAN: THEREFORE HE WILL NOT SPARE IN THE DAY OF VENGEANCE.

HE WILL NOT REGARD ANY RANSOM; NEITHER WILL HE REST CONTENT, THOUGH THOU GIVEST MANY GIFTS.

10

A GRACIOUS WOMAN RETAINS HONOR: AND THE STRONG RETAIN RICHES.

BY MICHAEL JAMES —

HE (SHE) THAT HAS A BOUNTIFUL EYE SHALL BE BLESSED; FOR HE (SHE) GIVES OF HIS (HER) BREAD TO THE POOR.

AN ANGRY MAN (WOMAN) STIRS UP STRIFE, AND A FURIOUS MAN (WOMAN) ABOUNDS IN TRANSGRESSION.

ART BY MICHAEL JAMES

PROVERBS 3:3-4; 11:16-19; 22:9; 29:22
MEGAN AND LEZLEEL TM MICHAEL JAMES

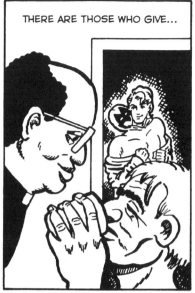

THERE ARE THOSE WHO GIVE...

AND YET INCREASE.

AND THERE ARE THOSE THAT WITHHOLD MORE THAN IS NECESSARY,

BUT IT LEADS TO POVERTY.

THE GENEROUS SOUL SHALL PROSPER,

AND HE WHO WATERS SHALL HIMSELF BE WATERED.

13

HE THAT HAS PITY UPON THE POOR, LENDS TO THE LORD.

AND THAT WHICH HE HAS GIVEN, WILL HE PAY HIM AGAIN.

HE THAT GIVES TO THE POOR SHALL NOT LACK,

BUT HE WHO HIDES HIS EYES SHALL HAVE MANY A CURSE.

HE THAT HAS A BOUNTIFUL EYE...

SHALL BE BLESSED;

FOR HE GIVES HIS BREAD TO THE POOR.

PROVERBS 11:24-25; 19:17; 28:27; 22:9

k.j.kolka '98

14

15

DO NOT OPPRESS THE AFFLICTED IN THE GATE:

FOR THE LORD WILL PLEAD THEIR CAUSE, AND SPOIL THE SOUL OF THOSE THAT SPOILED THEM.

16

AN ANGRY MAN STIRS UP DISSENSION,

AND A HOT TEMPERED ONE,

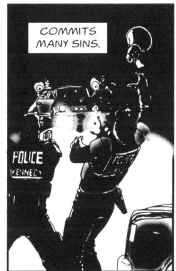

COMMITS MANY SINS.

IF YOU RESCUE HIM,

YOU WILL HAVE TO DO IT AGAIN.

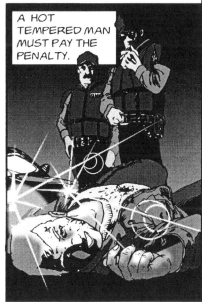

A HOT TEMPERED MAN MUST PAY THE PENALTY.

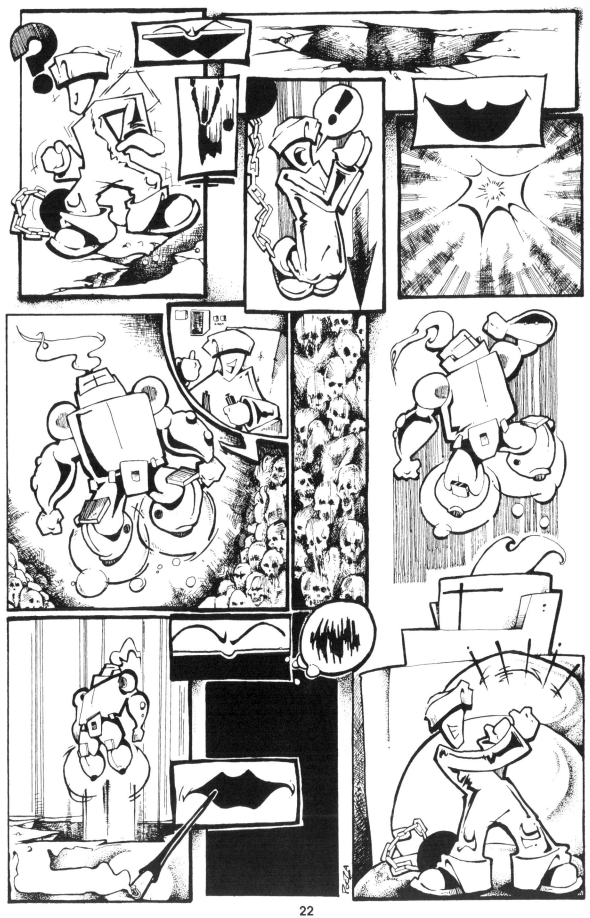

LAY NOT IN WAIT, O WICKED MAN, AGAINST THE DWELLING OF THE RIGHTEOUS...

FOR A JUST MAN FALLS SEVEN TIMES, AND RISES UP AGAIN,

BUT THE WICKED SHALL FALL BY CALAMITY.

REJOICE NOT WHEN YOUR ENEMY FALLS, AND LET NOT YOUR HEART BE GLAD WHEN HE STUMBLES:

LEST THE LORD SEE IT, AND IT DISPLEASES HIM,

AND HE TURN AWAY HIS WRATH FROM HIM.

ART BY MONTE WILSON

DO NOT FRET YOURSELF BECAUSE OF EVILDOERS, NEITHER BE ENVIOUS OF THE WICKED;
FOR THERE WILL BE NO FUTURE FOR THE EVIL MAN; THE LAMP OF THE WICKED WILL BE PUT OUT.

PROVERBS 24:15-20

WHO HAS WOE? WHO HAS SORROW? WHO HAS CONTENTIONS? WHO HAS BABBLING? WHO HAS WOUNDS WITHOUT CAUSE? WHO HAS REDNESS OF EYES?

THEY THAT TARRY LONG AT THE WINE; THEY THAT GO TO SEEK MIXED WINE. DO NOT LOOK AT THE WINE WHEN IT IS RED, WHEN IT SPARKLES IN THE CUP, WHEN IT GOES DOWN SMOOTHLY.

AT THE LAST IT BITES LIKE A SERPENT, AND STINGS LIKE AN ADDER. YOUR EYES SHALL BEHOLD STRANGE THINGS, AND YOUR HEART SHALL UTTER PERVERSE THINGS.

YEA, YOU SHALL BE AS UNSTEADY AS HE THAT LIES DOWN IN THE MIDST OF THE SEA, OR AS HE THAT LIES DOWN AT THE TOP OF THE MAST. YOU WILL SAY THEY HAVE STRUCK ME, AND I WAS NOT SICK; THEY HAVE BEATEN ME, AND I FELT IT NOT: WHEN SHALL I AWAKE? I WILL SEEK ANOTHER DRINK.

PROVERBS 23:29-35

AScoundrel&AVILLAIN...

WALKS WITH A PERVERSE MOUTH...

HE WINKS WITH HIS EYES...

...HE MOTIONS WITH HIS FINGERS...

...HE
SPEAKS
BY
TAPPING
HIS FEET...

ART BY HAL JONES

The Tongue

AS COALS ARE TO BURNING COALS, AND WOOD TO FIRE;

SO IS A CONTENTIOUS MAN TO KINDLE STRIFE.

THE WORDS OF A TALEBEARER ARE LIKE DAINTY MORSELS...

AND THEY GO DOWN INTO THE INNERMOST PARTS OF THE BELLY.

BURNING LIPS AND A WICKED HEART ARE LIKE AN EARTHEN VESSEL...

COVERED WITH GLAZE FROM MOLTEN SILVER.

ART BY BILLY LEAVELL

30

WHO CAN FIND A
VIRTUOUS WOMAN?
FOR HER PRICE IS FAR
ABOVE RUBIES.

SHE IS LIKE THE
MERCHANTS' SHIPS;
SHE BRINGETH HER
FOOD FROM AFAR.

SHE RISETH ALSO WHILE
IT IS YET NIGHT, AND
GIVETH MEAT TO HER
HOUSEHOLD.

SHE CONSIDERETH THE
FIELD, AND BUYETH IT:
WITH THE FRUIT OF HER
HANDS SHE PLANTETH A
VINEYARD.

SHE GIRDS HERSELF
WITH STRENGTH, AND
STRENGTHENETH HER
ARMS.

SHE LAYETH HER HANDS
TO THE SPINDLE, AND
HER HANDS HOLD THE
DISTAFF.

ART BY KATHLEEN WEBB

SHE STRETCHETH OUT HER HAND TO THE POOR; YEA, SHE REACHETH FORTH HER HANDS TO THE NEEDY.

SHE MAKETH FINE LINEN, AND SELLETH IT, AND DELIVERETH GIRDLES UNTO THE MERCHANT.

STRENGTH AND HONOR ARE HER CLOTHING; AND SHE SHALL REJOICE IN TIME TO COME.

SHE OPENS HER MOUTH WITH WISDOM; AND IN HER TONGUE IS THE LAW OF KINDNESS.

HER CHILDREN ARISE UP, AND CALL HER BLESSED; HER HUSBAND ALSO, AND HE PRAISES HER.

CHARM IS DECEITFUL, AND BEAUTY IS VAIN: BUT A WOMAN THAT FEARETH THE LORD, SHE SHALL BE PRAISED.

·AMEN·

32

PROVERBS 31:10-30

PROVERBS 23:4-5

33

ART BY CARLOS GARZON

MAKE NO FRIENDSHIP WITH AN ANGRY MAN,

AND WITH A FURIOUS MAN YOU SHALL NOT GO,

LEST YOU LEARN HIS WAYS,

AND GET YOURSELF INTO A SNARE.

PROVERBS 22:24-25

34

ART BY FAREL DALRYMPLE

35

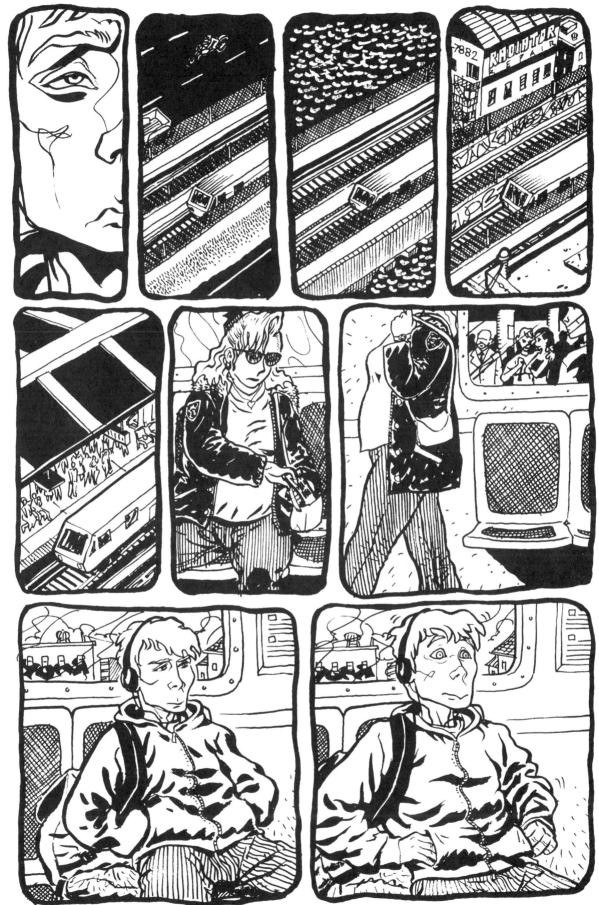

...DELIVER THEM THAT ARE DRAWN UNTO DEATH, AND THOSE THAT ARE READY TO BE SLAIN. IF YOU SAY, BEHOLD, WE DID NOT KNOW IT; DOES NOT HE THAT PONDERS THE HEART CONSIDER IT? AND HE THAT KEEPS YOUR SOUL, DOES HE NOT KNOW IT? AND SHALL HE NOT RENDER TO EVERY MAN ACCORDING TO HIS WORKS?

PROVERBS 24:11-12

Dear Son...

FOR AT THE WINDOW OF MY HOUSE I LOOKED THROUGH MY LATTICE,

AND BEHELD AMONG THE SIMPLE ONES, I DISCERNED AMONG THE YOUTHS, A YOUNG MAN VOID OF UNDERSTANDING,

PASSING THROUGH THE STREET NEAR HER CORNER;

AND HE WENT THE WAY TO HER HOUSE.

ART BY GEOFF STROUT

AND BEHOLD, THERE A WOMAN MET HIM...

...WITH THE ATTIRE OF A HARLOT AND CUNNING OF HEART.

SHE IS LOUD AND STUBBORN; HER FEET STAY NOT IN HER HOUSE:

SHE IS NOW IN THE STREETS, AND LIES IN WAIT AT EVERY CORNER.

SO SHE CAUGHT HIM,

...AND KISSED HIM

...AND WITH AN IMPUDENT FACE SAID UNTO HIM,

...I CAME FORTH TO MEET YOU, DILIGENTLY TO SEEK YOUR FACE AND I HAVE FOUND YOU.

I HAVE SPREAD MY BED WITH FINE LINEN OF EGYPT.

I HAVE PERFUMED MY BED WITH MYRRH, ALOES AND CINNAMON.

COME, LET US TAKE OUR FILL OF LOVE UNTIL THE MORNING: LET US DELIGHT OURSELVES WITH LOVE.

FOR THE MAN IS NOT HOME, HE IS GONE ON A LONG JOURNEY.

HE HAS TAKEN A BAG OF MONEY WITH HIM, AND WILL COME HOME AT THE FULL MOON.

WITH HER ENTICING SPEECH SHE CAUSED HIM TO YIELD, WITH THE FLATTERING OF HER LIPS SHE FORCED HIM.

SUDDENLY HE FOLLOWED HER,

AS AN OX GOES...

...TO THE SLAUGHTER.

...OR AS A FOOL...

...TO THE CORRECTION OF THE STOCKS.

...AS A BIRD HASTENS TO THE SNARE.

...NOT KNOWING

THAT IT WILL COST

HIS LIFE.

LET NOT YOUR HEART INCLINE TO HER WAYS, DO NOT STRAY IN HER PATH.

FOR SHE HAS CAST DOWN MANY WOUNDED:

YES, MANY STRONG MEN HAVE BEEN SLAIN BY HER.

HER HOUSE IS THE WAY TO HELL,

GOING DOWN TO THE CHAMBERS OF DEATH.

In Sincere Warning Your Father

42

the **arrogance** of Man (PROVERBS 30:11-17)

illustrated by kenn bivins

MONOCLE GENETICS INC.

HOW TO MAKE MAN IN 5 DAYS

THERE ARE THOSE WHO CURSE THEIR FATHERS AND DO NOT BLESS THEIR MOTHERS

THOSE WHO ARE PURE IN THEIR OWN EYES AND YET ARE NOT CLEANSED OF THEIR FILTH

THE LEECH HAS TWO DAUGHTERS. "GIVE! GIVE!," THEY CRY.

THERE ARE THREE THINGS THAT ARE NEVER SATISFIED,

FOUR THAT NEVER SAY, "ENOUGH!"

THE GRAVE,

THE BARREN WOMB,

LAND WHICH IS NEVER SATISFIED WITH WATER,

DANGER!!! SECURITY LOCKS DISABLED EVACUATE!!!

AND FIRE WHICH NEVER SAYS, "ENOUGH!"

THE EYE THAT MOCKS A FATHER, THAT SCORNS OBEDIENCE TO A MOTHER,

WILL BE PECKED OUT BY THE RAVENS OF THE VALLEY, AND WILL BE EATEN BY THE VULTURES.

45

PENCILS BY DEVIN PARKER
INKS BY GREG DAMPIER, JESSE HAMM & RALPH ELLIS MILEY

GET WISDOM; GET UNDERSTANDING: FORGET IT NOT; NEITHER DECLINE FROM THE WORDS OF MY MOUTH. FORSAKE HER NOT, AND SHE SHALL PRESERVE THEE: LOVE HER, AND SHE WILL KEEP THEE.

WISDOM IS THE PRINCIPAL THING; THEREFORE GET WISDOM: AND WITH ALL THY GETTING, GET UNDERSTANDING.

EXALT HER, AND SHE SHALL PROMOTE THEE:

SHE SHALL BRING THEE TO HONOR, WHEN THOU DOST EMBRACE HER.

SHE SHALL GIVE TO THINE HEAD AN ORNAMENT OF GRACE: A CROWN OF GLORY SHALL SHE DELIVER TO THEE.

HEAR, O MY SON, AND RECEIVE MY SAYINGS; AND THE YEARS OF THY LIFE SHALL BE MANY.

I HAVE TAUGHT THEE IN THE WAY OF WISDOM, I HAVE LED THEE IN RIGHT PATHS.

47

PROVERBS 9:1-9-13-18

 WISDOM HATH BUILDED HER HOUSE, SHE HATH HEWN OUT HER SEVEN PILLARS.

SHE HATH KILLED HER BEASTS; SHE HATH MINGLED HER WINE; SHE HATH ALSO FURNISHED HER TABLE.

SHE HATH SENT FORTH HER MAIDENS;

SHE CRIETH UPON THE HIGHEST PLACES OF THE CITY:

WHOSO IS SIMPLE LET HIM TURN HITHER!

As for him that wanteth understanding, she saith to him:

Forsake the foolish, and live! And go in the way of understanding!

He that reproveth a scorner getteth to himself shame: and he that rebuketh a wicked man getteth himself a blot.

Reprove not a scorner, lest he hate thee...

Rebuke a wise man and he will love thee...

Give instruction to a wise man, and he will increase in learning.

A FOOLISH WOMAN IS CLAMOROUS: SHE IS SIMPLE, AND KNOWETH NOTHING. FOR SHE SITTETH AT THE DOOR OF HER HOUSE, ON A SEAT IN THE HIGH PLACES OF THE CITY, TO CALL TO PASSENGERS WHO GO RIGHT ON THEIR WAYS:

WHOSO IS SIMPLE LET HIM TURN IN HERE!

AND AS FOR HIM THAT WANTETH UNDERSTANDING, SHE SAITH TO HIM:

STOLEN WATERS ARE SWEET, AND BREAD EATEN IN SECRET IS PLEASANT!

BUT HE KNOWETH NOT THAT THE DEAD ARE THERE...

AND THAT HER GUESTS ARE IN THE DEPTHS OF HELL.

RICHES AND HONOR ARE WITH ME, YEA, DURABLE RICHES AND RIGHTEOUSNESS. MY FRUIT IS BETTER THAN GOLD, YEA, FINE GOLD; AND MY REVENUE THAN CHOICE SILVER. I LEAD IN THE WAY OF RIGHTEOUSNESS, IN THE MIDST OF THE PATHS OF JUDGMENT... AND I WILL FILL THEIR TREASURES.

THE LORD POSSESSED ME IN THE BEGINNING OF HIS WAY, BEFORE HIS WORKS OF OLD. I WAS SET UP FROM EVERLASTING, FROM THE BEGINNING, OR EVER THE EARTH WAS. WHEN THERE WERE NO DEPTHS, I WAS BROUGHT FORTH; WHEN THERE WERE NO FOUNTAINS ABOUNDING WITH WATER. BEFORE THE MOUNTAINS WERE SETTLED, BEFORE THE HILLS WAS I BROUGHT FORTH: WHILE AS YET HE HAD NOT MADE THE EARTH, NOR THE FIELDS, NOR THE HIGHEST PART OF THE DUST OF THE WORLD. WHEN HE PREPARED THE HEAVENS, I WAS THERE: WHEN HE SET A COMPASS UPON THE FACE OF THE DEPTH:

WHEN HE ESTABLISHED THE CLOUDS ABOVE: WHEN HE STRENGTHENED THE FOUNDATIONS OF THE DEEP: WHEN HE GAVE TO THE SEA HIS DECREE, THAT THE WATERS SHOULD NOT PASS HIS COMMANDMENT: WHEN HE APPOINTED THE FOUNDATIONS OF THE EARTH:

THEN WAS I BY HIM, AS ONE BROUGHT UP WITH HIM: AND I WAS DAILY HIS DELIGHT, REJOICING ALWAYS BEFORE HIM; REJOICING IN THE HABITABLE PART OF HIS EARTH; AND MY DELIGHTS WERE WITH THE SONS OF MEN.

NOW THEREFORE HARKEN UNTO ME, O YE CHILDREN: FOR BLESSED ARE THEY THAT KEEP MY WAYS.

THE FEAR OF THE LORD IS THE BEGINNING OF WISDOM: AND THE KNOWLEDGE OF THE HOLY IS UNDERSTANDING. FOR BY ME THY DAYS SHALL BE MULTIPLIED, AND THE YEARS OF THY LIFE SHALL BE INCREASED. IF THOU BE WISE, THOU SHALT BE WISE FOR THYSELF: BUT IF THOU SCORNEST, THOU ALONE SHALT BEAR IT.

HEAR INSTRUCTION, AND BE WISE, AND REFUSE IT NOT. BLESSED IS THE MAN THAT HEARETH ME, WATCHING DAILY AT MY GATES, WAITING AT THE POSTS OF MY DOORS. FOR WHOSO FINDETH ME FINDETH LIFE, AND SHALL OBTAIN FAVOR OF THE LORD.

PROVERBS 4:1-11, 8:13-35, 9:10-12

OTHER SCRIPTURES

54

"BEHOLD, I WAS BROUGHT **FORTH** IN INIQUITY, AND IN SIN MY MOTHER CONCEIVED ME. BEHOLD, YOU DESIRE **TRUTH** IN THE INWARD PARTS, AND IN THE HIDDEN PART YOU WILL MAKE ME TO KNOW **WISDOM**.

"PURGE ME WITH HYSSOP, AND I SHALL BE **CLEAN**; WASH ME AND I SHALL BE **WHITER** THAN SNOW.

"MAKE ME TO **HEAR** JOY AND GLADNESS, THAT THE BONES WHICH YOU HAVE BROKEN MAY **REJOICE**. HIDE YOUR FACE FROM MY SINS, AND BLOT OUT **ALL** MY INIQUITIES.

"CREATE IN ME A **CLEAN** HEART, O GOD, AND RENEW A STEADFAST **SPIRIT** WITHIN ME. DO NOT CAST ME AWAY FROM YOUR **PRESENCE**, AND DO **NOT** TAKE YOUR HOLY SPIRIT FROM ME.

"RESTORE TO ME THE **JOY** OF YOUR SALVATION, AND **UPHOLD** ME WITH YOUR GENEROUS SPIRIT. THEN I WILL **TEACH** TRANSGRESSORS YOUR WAYS, AND **SINNERS** WILL BE CONVERTED TO YOU."

ART BY SERGIO CARIELLO

THERE IS A SORE EVIL WHICH I HAVE SEEN UNDER THE SUN,...

...NAMELY, RICHES KEPT FOR THE OWNERS TO THEIR HURT.

BUT THOSE RICHES PERISH BY EVIL TRAVAIL:...

...AND HE HAS A SON, AND THERE IS NOTHING IN HIS HAND.

AND AS HE CAME FORTH FROM HIS MOTHER'S WOMB,

NAKED SHALL HE RETURN TO GO AS HE CAME...

AND SHALL TAKE NOTHING OF HIS LABOR, WHICH HE MAY CARRY AWAY IN HIS HAND.

ART BY MARK AMMERMAN

TWO ARE BETTER THAN ONE;

BECAUSE THEY HAVE A GOOD REWARD FOR THEIR LABOR.

FOR IF THEY FALL,

THE ONE WILL LIFT UP HIS FELLOW.

ECCLESIASTES 4:8-12

A FRIEND LOVES AT ALL TIMES, AND A BROTHER IS BORN FOR ADVERSITY. --PROVERBS 17:17

Thou art the Potter...

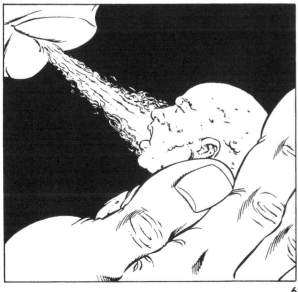

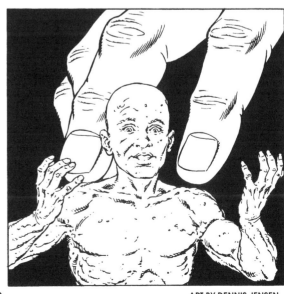

ART BY DENNIS JENSEN

~~~ I am the clay ~~~

BUT NOW, O LORD, THOU ART OUR FATHER; WE ARE THE CLAY, AND THOU OUR
POTTER; AND WE ALL ARE THE WORK OF THY HAND. ISAIAH 64:8

AGAIN THE WORD OF THE LORD CAME TO ME SAYING, SON OF MAN, SPEAK TO THE CHILDREN OF YOUR PEOPLE AND SAY UNTO THEM, WHEN I BRING THE SWORD UPON THE LAND, IF THE PEOPLE OF THE LAND TAKE A MAN OF THEIR COASTS, AND SIT HIM FOR THEIR WATCHMAN:

IF WHEN HE SEES THE SWORD COME UPON THE LAND, HE BLOW THE TRUMPET, AND WARN THE PEOPLE;

THEN WHOEVER HEARS THE SOUND OF THE TRUMPET, AND TAKES NOT WARNING; IF THE SWORD COME, AND TAKES HIM AWAY, HIS BLOOD SHALL BE UPON HIS OWN HEAD.

HE HEARD THE SOUND OF THE TRUMPET, AND TOOK NOT THE WARNING; HIS BLOOD SHALL BE UPON HIM. BUT HE THAT TOOK THE WARNING SHALL DELIVER HIS SOUL.

ART BY BILL WEBB   EZEKIEL 33:1-9

BUT IF THE WATCHMAN SEE THE SWORD COME, AND BLOW NOT THE TRUMPET, AND THE PEOPLE BE NOT WARNED; IF THE SWORD COME, AND TAKE ANY PERSON FROM THEM, HE IS TAKEN AWAY IN HIS INIQUITY...

...BUT HIS BLOOD WILL I REQUIRE AT THE WATCHMAN'S HAND.

SO THOU, O SON OF MAN, I HAVE SET A WATCHMAN... THEREFORE YOU SHALL HEAR THE WORD AT MY MOUTH, AND WARN THEM FROM ME.

WHEN I SAY UNTO THE WICKED, O WICKED MAN, YOU SHALL SURELY DIE; IF YOU DO NOT SPEAK TO WARN THE WICKED FROM HIS WAY, THAT WICKED MAN SHALL DIE IN HIS INIQUITY; BUT HIS BLOOD WILL I REQUIRE AT YOUR HAND.

NEVERTHELESS, IF YOU WARN THE WICKED OF HIS WAY TO TURN FROM IT; IF HE DID NOT TURN FROM HIS WAY, HE SHALL DIE IN HIS INIQUITY; BUT YOU HAVE DELIVERED YOUR SOUL.

PARABLES

HE ANSWERED AND SAID UNTO THEM, HE THAT SOWS THE GOOD SEED IS THE SON OF MAN; THE FIELD IS THE WORLD; THE GOOD SEED ARE THE CHILDREN OF THE KINGDOM; BUT THE TARES ARE THE CHILDREN OF THE WICKED ONE; THE ENEMY THAT SOWED THEM IS THE DEVIL; THE HARVEST IS THE END OF THE WORLD; AND THE REAPERS ARE THE ANGELS.

ART BY LEO BAK

AS THE TARES

ARE GATHERED

AND BURNED
IN THE FIRE,

SO SHALL IT BE IN THE
END OF THIS WORLD.
THE SON OF MAN SHALL
SEND FORTH HIS
ANGELS,

AND THEY SHALL GATHER OUT OF HIS KINGDOM ALL CAUSES OF OFFENSE, AND THEM WHICH DO EVIL;

AND SHALL CAST THEM INTO THE FURNACE OF FIRE:

THERE SHALL BE WAILING AND GNASHING OF TEETH.

THEN SHALL THE RIGHTEOUS SHINE FORTH AS THE SUN IN THE KINGDOM OF THEIR FATHER.

HE WHO HAS EARS TO HEAR, LET HIM HEAR.

70

MATTHEW 13:37-43

ENTER THROUGH THE
NARROW GATE; FOR WIDE
IS THE GATE, AND BROAD
IS THE WAY THAT LEADS
TO DESTRUCTION, AND
MANY THERE BE THAT ENTER
IN. BECAUSE NARROW IS THE
GATE, AND NARROW IS THE
WAY, WHICH LEADS TO LIFE,
AND FEW THERE BE THAT
FIND IT.

ART BY ROMAN MORALES III

BEWARE OF FALSE PROPHETS, WHICH COME TO YOU IN SHEEP'S CLOTHING, BUT INWARDLY THEY ARE RAVENOUS WOLVES.

YOU SHALL KNOW THEM BY THEIR FRUITS.

A GOOD TREE CANNOT BRING FORTH EVIL FRUIT, NEITHER CAN A CORRUPT TREE BRING FORTH GOOD FRUIT.

NOT EVERYONE THAT SAYS TO ME, LORD, LORD SHALL ENTER INTO THE KINGDOM OF HEAVEN; BUT HE THAT DOES THE WILL OF MY FATHER WHICH IS IN HEAVEN. MANY WILL SAY TO ME IN THAT DAY, LORD, LORD, HAVE WE NOT PROPHESIED IN YOUR NAME? AND IN YOUR NAME CAST OUT DEVILS? AND IN YOUR NAME DONE MANY WONDERFUL WORKS?

WHEREFORE BY THEIR FRUITS YOU SHALL KNOW THEM.

AND THEN I WILL PROFESS TO THEM, I NEVER KNEW YOU: DEPART FROM ME, YOU THAT WORK INIQUITY.

MATTHEW 7:13-23

THEREFORE WHOSOEVER HEARETH THESE SAYINGS OF MINE, AND DOETH THEM, I WILL LIKEN HIM UNTO A WISE MAN, WHICH BUILT HIS HOUSE UPON A ROCK:

AND THE RAIN DESCENDED...

...AND THE FLOODS CAME...

...AND THE WINDS BLEW, AND BEAT UPON THAT HOUSE...

...AND IT FELL NOT: FOR IT WAS FOUNDED UPON A ROCK.

PENCILS BY G. RAYMOND EDDY
INKS BY MICHAEL JAMES

AND EVERY ONE THAT HEARETH THESE SAYINGS OF MINE, AND DOETH THEM NOT, SHALL BE LIKENED UNTO A FOOLISH MAN, WHICH BUILT HIS HOUSE UPON THE SAND.

AND THE RAIN DESCENDED...

...AND THE FLOODS CAME...

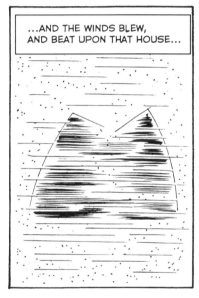

...AND THE WINDS BLEW, AND BEAT UPON THAT HOUSE...

...AND IT FELL: AND GREAT WAS THE FALL OF IT.

George Raymond Eddy

MATTHEW 7:24-27

AND WHEN MANY PEOPLE WERE GATHERED TOGETHER AND CAME TO HIM OUT OF EVERY CITY, HE SPOKE A PARABLE:

A SOWER WENT OUT TO SOW HIS SEED:

AND AS HE SOWED, SOME FELL BY THE WAY SIDE; AND IT WAS TRODDEN DOWN, AND THE FOWLS OF THE AIR DEVOURED IT.

AND SOME FELL UPON A ROCK; AND AS SOON AS IT WAS SPRUNG UP, IT WITHERED AWAY, BECAUSE IT LACKED MOISTURE.

AND SOME FELL AMONG THORNS AND THE THORNS SPRANG UP WITH IT, AND CHOKED IT.

AND OTHER FELL ON GOOD GROUND, AND SPRANG UP, AND BARE FRUIT, A HUNDREDFOLD.

AND HIS DISCIPLES ASKED HIM, SAYING, "WHAT MIGHT THIS PARABLE BE?"

ART BY BUD ROGERS

NOW THE PARABLE IS THIS:

THE SEED IS THE WORD OF GOD.

THOSE BY THE WAY SIDE ARE THEY THAT HEAR; THEN COMES THE DEVIL, AND TAKES AWAY THE WORD OUT OF THEIR HEARTS, LEST THEY SHOULD BELIEVE AND BE SAVED.

THEY ON THE ROCK ARE THOSE, WHEN THEY HEAR, RECEIVE THE WORD WITH JOY; AND THESE HAVE NO ROOT, WHICH FOR A WHILE BELIEVE, AND IN TIME OF TEMPTATION FALL AWAY.

AND THAT WHICH FELL AMONG THE THORNS ARE THEY, WHICH, WHEN THEY HAVE HEARD, GO FORTH, AND ARE CHOKED WITH CARES AND RICHES AND PLEASURES OF THIS LIFE, AND BRING NO FRUIT TO MATURITY.

BUT THAT ON THE GOOD GROUND ARE THEY, WHICH IN AN HONEST AND GOOD HEART, HAVING HEARD THE WORD, KEEP IT, AND BRING FORTH FRUIT WITH PATIENCE.

B. ROGERS '79

LUKE 8:4-8A, 9, 11-15

AGAIN, THE KINGDOM OF HEAVEN IS LIKE UNTO A NET, THAT WAS CAST INTO THE SEA, AND GATHERED OF EVERY KIND:

WHICH, WHEN IT WAS FULL, THEY DREW TO SHORE, AND SAT DOWN, AND GATHERED THE GOOD INTO VESSELS, BUT CAST THE BAD AWAY.

ART BY EDDIE EDDINGS

SO SHALL IT BE AT THE END OF THE WORLD: THE ANGELS SHALL COME FORTH, AND SEVER THE WICKED FROM AMONG THE JUST, AND SHALL CAST THEM INTO THE FURNACE OF FIRE: THERE SHALL BE WAILING AND GNASHING OF TEETH.

MATTHEW 13:47-50

FOR THE KINGDOM OF HEAVEN IS LIKE UNTO A MAN THAT IS A LANDOWNER, WHO WENT OUT EARLY IN THE MORNING TO HIRE LABORERS INTO HIS VINEYARD.

AND WHEN HE HAD AGREED WITH THE LABORERS FOR A PENNY A DAY, HE SENT THEM INTO HIS VINEYARD. AND HE WENT OUT ABOUT THE THIRD HOUR, AND SAW OTHERS STANDING IDLE IN THE MARKETPLACE, AND HE SAID UNTO THEM, GO ALSO INTO THE VINEYARD, AND WHATEVER IS RIGHT I WILL GIVE YOU. AND THEY WENT THEIR WAY.

AGAIN HE WENT OUT ABOUT THE SIXTH AND NINTH HOUR, AND DID LIKEWISE.

AND ABOUT THE ELEVENTH HOUR HE WENT OUT, AND FOUND OTHERS STANDING IDLE...

...AND SAID UNTO THEM, WHY DO YOU STAND HERE ALL THE DAY IDLE? THEY SAID UNTO HIM, BECAUSE NO MAN HAS HIRED US. HE SAID UNTO THEM, GO ALSO INTO THE VINEYARD; AND WHATEVER IS RIGHT, THAT SHALL YOU RECEIVE.

PENCILS BY KYLE VANNOY
INKS BY PETER SFAT

SO WHEN EVENING HAD COME, THE LORD OF THE VINEYARD SAID UNTO HIS FOREMAN, CALL THE LABORERS, AND GIVE THEM THEIR WAGES, BEGINNING FROM THE LAST UNTO THE FIRST.

AND WHEN THEY CAME THAT WERE HIRED ABOUT THE ELEVENTH HOUR, THEY RECEIVED EVERY MAN A PENNY.

BUT WHEN THE FIRST CAME, THEY SUPPOSED THAT THEY SHOULD HAVE RECEIVED MORE; AND THEY LIKEWISE RECEIVED EVERY MAN A PENNY. AND WHEN THEY HAD RECEIVED IT, THEY MURMURED AGAINST THE LANDOWNER.

SAYING, THESE LAST HAVE WORKED BUT ONE HOUR, AND YOU HAVE MADE THEM EQUAL UNTO US, WHO HAVE BORNE THE BURDEN AND HEAT OF THE DAY.

BUT HE ANSWERED ONE OF THEM, AND SAID, FRIEND, I DID YOU NO WRONG: DID YOU NOT AGREE WITH ME FOR ONE PENNY? TAKE IT AND GO YOUR WAY: I WILL GIVE UNTO LAST, EVEN AS UNTO YOU. IS IT NOT LAWFUL FOR ME TO DO WHAT I WILL WITH MY OWN MONEY? IS YOUR EYE EVIL BECAUSE I AM GOOD?

SO SHALL THE LAST BE FIRST, AND THE FIRST LAST: FOR MANY ARE CALLED, BUT FEW CHOSEN.

"TWO SONS"

BUT WHAT THINK YE? A CERTAIN MAN HAD TWO SONS; AND HE CAME TO THE FIRST,

AND SAID,

SON, GO WORK TODAY IN MY YARD.

HE ANSWERED AND SAID,

I WILL NOT:

BUT AFTERWARD HE REPENTED,

AND WENT.

AND HE CAME TO THE SECOND, AND SAID LIKEWISE. AND HE ANSWERED AND SAID,

I GO SIR:

AND WENT NOT.

ART BY ANDRE SZYMANOWICZ

MATTHEW 21:28-32

"LISTEN TO ANOTHER PARABLE: THERE WAS A LANDOWNER WHO PLANTED A VINEYARD."

MATTHEW 21: 33-46

"HE PUT A WALL AROUND IT, DUG A WINEPRESS IN IT, AND BUILT A WATCHTOWER. THEN HE RENTED THE VINEYARD TO SOME FARMERS AND WENT AWAY ON A JOURNEY."

"WHEN THE HARVEST TIME APPROACHED, HE SENT HIS SERVANTS TO COLLECT HIS FRUIT.

THE TENANTS SEIZED HIS SERVANTS; THEY BEAT ONE,...

... KILLED ANOTHER,...

... AND STONED A THIRD."

"THEN HE SENT OTHER SERVANTS, MORE THAN THE FIRST TIME, AND THE TENANTS TREATED THEM THE SAME WAY."

ART BY TODD TENNANT

"LAST OF ALL, HE SENT HIS SON TO THEM. "THEY WILL RESPECT MY SON," HE SAID."

"BUT WHEN THE TENANTS SAW THE SON, THEY SAID TO EACH OTHER, "THIS IS THE HEIR. COME, LET'S KILL HIM AND TAKE HIS INHERITANCE." SO THEY TOOK HIM AND THREW HIM OUT OF THE VINEYARD AND KILLED HIM."

"THEREFORE, WHEN THE OWNER OF THE VINEYARD COMES, WHAT WILL HE DO TO THOSE TENANTS?" "HE WILL BRING THOSE WRETCHES TO A WRETCHED END," THEY REPLIED, "AND HE WILL RENT THE VINEYARD TO OTHER TENANTS, WHO WILL GIVE HIM HIS SHARE OF THE CROP AT HARVEST TIME."

JESUS THEN SAID TO THEM, "HAVE YOU NEVER READ IN THE SCRIPTURES : '*THE STONE THE BUILDERS REJECTED HAS BECOME THE CAPSTONE ; THE LORD HAS DONE THIS, AND IT IS MARVELOUS IN OUR EYES*' ?"

"THEREFORE I TELL YOU THAT THE KINGDOM OF GOD WILL BE TAKEN AWAY FROM YOU AND GIVEN TO A PEOPLE WHO WILL PRODUCE ITS FRUIT. HE WHO FALLS ON THIS STONE WILL BE BROKEN TO PIECES, BUT HE ON WHOM IT FALLS WILL BE CRUSHED."

WHEN THE CHIEF PRIESTS AND THE PHARISEES HEARD JESUS' PARABLES, THEY KNEW HE WAS TALKING ABOUT THEM. THEY LOOKED FOR A WAY TO ARREST HIM, BUT THEY WERE AFRAID OF THE CROWD BECAUSE THE PEOPLE HELD THAT HE WAS A PROPHET.

THE PARABLE OF THE TEN VIRGINS

THEN SHALL THE KINGDOM OF HEAVEN BE LIKENED UNTO TEN VIRGINS, WHICH TOOK THEIR LAMPS, AND WENT FORTH TO MEET THE BRIDEGROOM.

AND FIVE OF THEM WERE WISE, AND FIVE WERE FOOLISH.

THEY THAT WERE FOOLISH TOOK THEIR LAMPS, AND TOOK NO OIL WITH THEM: BUT THE WISE TOOK OIL IN THEIR VESSELS WITH THEIR LAMPS.

WHILE THE BRIDEGROOM TARRIED, THEY ALL SLUMBERED AND SLEPT.

AND AT MIDNIGHT THERE WAS A CRY HEARD, "BEHOLD, THE BRIDEGROOM COMES; GO OUT TO MEET HIM!"

THEN ALL THOSE VIRGINS AROSE, AND TRIMMED THEIR LAMPS.

ART BY ALEC STEVENS

AND THE FOOLISH SAID UNTO THE WISE, "GIVE US SOME OF YOUR OIL, FOR OUR LAMPS ARE GOING OUT!"

BUT THE WISE ANSWERED, SAYING, "NO, LEST THERE NOT BE ENOUGH FOR US AND YOU, BUT GO RATHER TO THEM WHO SELL, AND BUY FOR YOURSELVES."

AND WHILE THEY WENT TO BUY, THE BRIDEGROOM CAME, AND THOSE WHO WERE READY WENT IN WITH HIM TO THE MARRIAGE, AND THE DOOR WAS SHUT.

AFTERWARD CAME ALSO THE OTHER VIRGINS, SAYING, "LORD, LORD, OPEN TO US!"

BUT HE ANSWERED, "TRULY I SAY UNTO YOU, I KNOW YOU NOT."

WATCH THEREFORE, FOR YOU KNOW NEITHER THE DAY NOR THE HOUR WHEREIN THE SON OF MAN IS COMING.

ART BY JOSHUA D. RAY

AND HE SPOKE THIS PARABLE UNTO THEM SAYING,

WHAT MAN OF YOU, HAVING A HUNDRED SHEEP,

IF HE LOSES ONE OF THEM,

DOES NOT LEAVE THE NINETY-NINE IN THE WILDERNESS, AND GO AFTER THAT WHICH IS LOST, UNTIL HE FIND IT?

AND WHEN HE HAS FOUND IT, HE LAYS IT ON HIS SHOULDERS, REJOICING.

I SAY UNTO YOU, THAT LIKEWISE JOY SHALL BE IN HEAVEN OVER ONE SINNER THAT REPENTS, MORE THAN OVER NINETY-NINE JUST PERSONS, WHO NEED NO REPENTANCE.

AND WHEN HE COMES HOME, HE CALLS TOGETHER HIS FRIENDS AND NEIGHBORS, SAYING UNTO THEM, "REJOICE WITH ME, FOR I HAVE MY SHEEP WHICH WAS LOST."

LUKE 15:3-7

ART BY FAREL DALRYMPLE

ART BY GARY MARTIN

AND JESUS ANSWERING SAID: "A CERTAIN MAN WENT DOWN FROM JERUSALEM TO JERICHO, AND FELL AMONG THIEVES...

...WHO STRIPPED HIM OF HIS CLOTHING, AND WOUNDED HIM, AND DEPARTED, LEAVING HIM HALF DEAD. AND BY CHANCE THERE CAME A CERTAIN PRIEST THAT WAY: AND WHEN HE SAW HIM, HE PASSED BY ON THE OTHER SIDE. AND LIKEWISE A LEVITE, WHEN HE WAS AT THE PLACE, CAME AND LOOKED ON HIM, AND PASSED BY ON THE OTHER SIDE.

BUT A CERTAIN SAMARITAN AS HE JOURNEYED, CAME WHERE HE WAS: AND WHEN HE SAW HIM...

93

ART BY MIKE S. MILLER

...HE HAD COMPASSION ON HIM, AND WENT TO HIM, AND BOUND UP HIS WOUNDS, POURING IN OIL AND WINE...

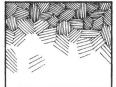

NOW WHICH OF THESE THREE DO YOU THINK WAS A NEIGHBOR TO HIM THAT FELL AMONG THE THIEVES?" AND HE SAID, "HE THAT SHOWED MERCY ON HIM." THEN JESUS SAID TO HIM, "GO AND DO LIKEWISE."

...AND SET HIM ON HIS OWN BEAST...

...AND BROUGHT HIM TO AN INN, AND TOOK CARE OF HIM.

AND THE NEXT DAY WHEN HE DEPARTED, HE TOOK OUT TWO PENCE, AND GAVE THEM TO THE HOST, AND SAID TO HIM, TAKE CARE OF HIM; AND WHATEVER MORE YOU SPEND, WHEN I COME AGAIN, I WILL REPAY YOU.

94

THE RICH MAN WITH MANY BARNS

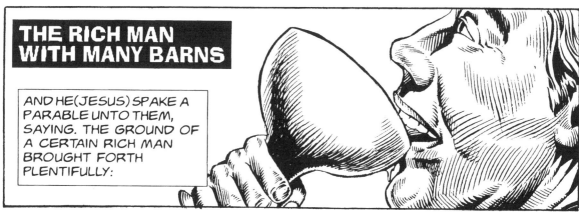

AND HE (JESUS) SPAKE A PARABLE UNTO THEM, SAYING. THE GROUND OF A CERTAIN RICH MAN BROUGHT FORTH PLENTIFULLY:

AND HE THOUGHT WITHIN HIMSELF SAYING, WHAT SHALL I DO BECAUSE I HAVE NO ROOM WHERE TO BESTOW MY FRUITS?

AND HE SAID, THIS WILL I DO: I WILL PULL DOWN MY BARNS, AND BUILD GREATER; AND THERE WILL I BESTOW ALL MY FRUITS AND MY GOODS.

95

PENCILS BY DON ENSIGN
INKS BY DANNY BULANADI

AND I WILL SAY TO MY SOUL, SOUL, THOU HAST MUCH GOODS LAID UP FOR MANY YEARS; TAKE THINE EASE, EAT, DRINK AND BE MERRY...

BUT GOD SAID UNTO HIM, THOU FOOL, THIS NIGHT THY SOUL SHALL BE REQUIRED OF THEE: THEN WHOSE SHALL THOSE THINGS BE WHICH THOU HAST PROVIDED?

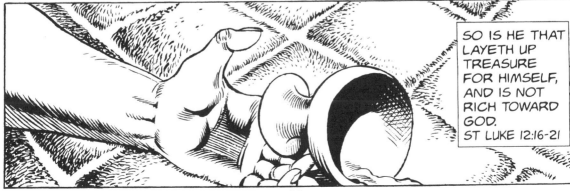

SO IS HE THAT LAYETH UP TREASURE FOR HIMSELF, AND IS NOT RICH TOWARD GOD.
ST LUKE 12:16-21

SUPPOSE ONE OF YOU HAS A FRIEND, AND HE GOES TO HIM AT MIDNIGHT AND SAYS,

FRIEND, LEND ME THREE LOAVES OF BREAD, BECAUSE A FRIEND OF MINE ON A JOURNEY HAS COME TO ME, AND I HAVE NOTHING TO SET BEFORE HIM.

DON'T BOTHER ME, THE DOOR IS ALREADY LOCKED, AND MY CHILDREN ARE WITH ME IN BED. I CAN'T GET UP AND GIVE YOU ANYTHING.

I TELL YOU, THOUGH HE WILL NOT GET UP AND GIVE HIM THE BREAD BECAUSE HE IS A FRIEND,

BANG
BANG
BANG

ART BY HAROLD BUCHHOLZ

YET BECAUSE OF THE MAN'S BOLDNESS HE WILL GET UP AND GIVE HIM AS MUCH AS HE NEEDS.

SO I SAY TO YOU: ASK AND IT WILL BE GIVEN TO YOU;

SEEK AND YOU WILL FIND;

KNOCK AND THE DOOR WILL BE OPENED TO YOU.

FOR EVERYONE WHO ASKS, RECEIVES;

HE WHO SEEKS, FINDS;

AND TO HIM WHO KNOCKS, THE DOOR WILL BE OPENED.

LUKE 11:5-10

ART BY MARK POE

AND HE PUT FORTH A PARABLE TO THOSE WHICH WERE INVITED, WHEN HE NOTICED HOW THEY CHOSE OUT THE CHIEF ROOMS; SAYING UNTO THEM,

WHEN YOU ARE INVITED TO A WEDDING FEAST,

...DO NOT SIT DOWN IN THE PLACE OF HONOR,

...LEST A MORE HONOR-ABLE MAN THAN YOU HAS BEEN INVITED.

AND HE WHO INVITED BOTH OF YOU COME TO YOU AND SAY,

YANK!

103

ART BY BILL MORRISON

ART BY CLINT JOHNSON

106

LUKE 14:16-24

ART BY CHRIS YAMBAR

OR WHAT KING, GOING TO MAKE WAR AGAINST ANOTHER, DOES NOT FIRST SIT DOWN...

...AND COUNSELS WHETHER HE IS ABLE WITH TEN THOUSAND TO MEET HIM THAT COMES AGAINST HIM WITH TWENTY THOUSAND.

FREE RESCUE MISSION DINNER TONIGHT.

RESCUE MISSION CLOSED TONIGHT. NO FUNDS.

SO LIKEWISE, WHOEVER OF YOU THAT FORSAKES NOT ALL HE HAS, HE CANNOT BE MY DISCIPLE.

SALT IS GOOD: BUT IF THE SALT HAS LOST HIS SAVOUR, WITH WHAT SHALL IT BE SEASONED?

CHARITY

IT IS NEITHER FIT FOR THE LAND, NOR FOR THE DUNGHILL; BUT MEN CAST IT OUT. HE THAT HAS EARS TO HEAR, LET HIM HEAR.

108

COUNTING THE COST!

FOR WHICH OF YOU, INTENDING TO BUILD A TOWER, SITTETH NOT DOWN FIRST, AND COUNTETH THE COST, WHETHER HE HAVE SUFFICIENT TO FINISH IT?

LEST HAPLY, AFTER HE HATH LAID THE FOUNDATION, AND IS NOT ABLE TO FINISH IT, ALL THAT BEHOLD IT BEGIN TO MOCK HIM,

SAYING, THIS MAN BEGAN TO BUILD, AND WAS NOT ABLE TO FINISH.

PENCILS- STEVEN BUTLER
INKS- NATE BUTLER

109

OR WHAT KING, GOING TO MAKE WAR AGAINST ANOTHER KING, SITTETH NOT DOWN FIRST, AND CONSULTETH WHETHER HE BE ABLE WITH TEN THOUSAND TO MEET HIM THAT COMETH AGAINST HIM WITH TWENTY THOUSAND?

OR ELSE, WHILE THE OTHER IS YET A GREAT WAY OFF, HE SENDETH AN AMBASSAGE, AND DESIRETH CONDITIONS OF PEACE.

SO LIKEWISE, WHOSOEVER HE BE OF YOU THAT FORSAKETH NOT ALL THAT HE HATH, HE CANNOT BE MY DISCIPLE.

SALT IS GOOD: BUT IF THE SALT HAVE LOST HIS SAVOUR, WHEREWITH SHALL IT BE SEASONED? IT IS NEITHER FIT FOR THE LAND, NOR YET FOR THE DUNGHILL; BUT MEN CAST IT OUT.

HE THAT HATH EARS TO HEAR, LET HIM HEAR.

LUKE 14 28-35

110

ART BY EDGAR WILLIAMS

ART BY GENE YANG

"The Pharisee stood and prayed thus with himself, 'God, I thank thee that I am not as other men are, extortioners, unjust, adulterers, or even as this tax collector. I fast twice in the week, I give tithes of all that I possess.'

"And the tax collector, standing at a distance, would not lift up so much as his eyes unto heaven, but beat upon his breast saying, 'God be merciful to me a sinner.'

"I tell you, this man went down to his house justified rather than the other: for everyone who exalts himself shall be humbled and he that humbleth himself shall be exalted."

Luke 18: 9 - 14

AND AS THEY HEARD THESE THINGS, HE ADDED AND SPOKE A PARABLE, BECAUSE THEY THOUGHT THAT THE KINGDOM OF GOD WAS GOING TO APPEAR IMMEDIATELY. HE SAID, A CERTAIN NOBLEMAN WENT INTO A FAR COUNTRY TO RECEIVE FOR HIMSELF A KINGDOM AND THEN RETURN. SO HE CALLED TEN OF HIS SERVANTS AND GAVE THEM TEN MINAS, AND SAID TO THEM, PUT THIS MONEY TO WORK UNTIL I RETURN. BUT HIS CITIZENS HATED HIM, AND SENT A MESSAGE AFTER HIM, SAYING, "WE WILL NOT HAVE THIS MAN REIGN OVER US.

GULP!

I SMACKER

AND IT CAME TO PASS, THAT WHEN HE RETURNED, HAVING RECEIVED THE KINGDOM, THEN HE COMMANDED THESE SERVANTS TO BE CALLED UNTO HIM, TO WHOM HE HAD GIVEN THE MONEY, THAT HE MIGHT KNOW HOW MUCH EVERY MAN HAD GAINED BY TRADING. THEN CAME THE FIRST, SAYING, LORD, YOUR MINA HAS GAINED TEN MINAS. AND HE SAID UNTO HIM, WELL DONE GOOD SERVANT: BECAUSE YOU HAVE BEEN FAITHFUL IN A VERY LITTLE, YOU SHALL HAVE AUTHORITY OVER TEN CITIES.

MASTER?

ONLY ONE SMACKER

SERVANT AL'S KOSHER HOT DOGS

AND THE SECOND MAN CAME SAYING, LORD, YOUR MINA HAS GAINED FIVE MINAS.

MASTER?

LEMONADE 50¢

117

AND HE SAID LIKEWISE TO HIM, YOU SHALL HAVE AUTHORITY OVER FIVE CITIES.

AND ANOTHER CAME, SAYING, LORD, BEHOLD, HERE IS YOUR MINA WHICH I HAVE KEPT LAID UP IN A CLOTH.

FOR I FEARED YOU, BECAUSE YOU ARE A HARD MAN, YOU PICK UP WHAT YOU DID NOT LAY DOWN, AND YOU REAP WHAT YOU DID NOT SOW. AND HE SAID UNTO HIM, "OUT OF YOUR OWN MOUTH WILL I JUDGE YOU, YOU WICKED SERVANT. YOU KNEW I WAS A HARD MAN, PICKING UP WHAT I DID NOT LAY DOWN, AND REAPING WHAT I DID NOT SOW: WHY THEN DID YOU NOT PUT MY MONEY INTO THE BANK, THAT AT MY COMING I MIGHT HAVE MY MONEY WITH SOME INTEREST? AND HE SAID TO THEM THAT STOOD BY, "TAKE FROM HIM THE MINA, AND GIVE IT TO HIM THAT HAS TEN MINAS."

AND THEY SAID UNTO HIM, LORD, HE HAS TEN MINAS. FOR I SAY UNTO YOU, THAT EVERYONE THAT HAS SHALL BE GIVEN MORE, AND FROM HIM THAT HAS NOT, EVEN THAT SHALL BE TAKEN AWAY FROM HIM. BUT MY ENEMIES WHO DID NOT WANT ME TO REIGN OVER THEM, BRING THEM HERE AND SLAY THEM BEFORE ME. LUKE 19:11-27

ART BY DAVID MURPHY AND MELISSA MURPHY

...THE GOOD SHEPHERD GIVES HIS LIFE FOR THE SHEEP.

BUT HE THAT IS AN HIRELING, AND NOT THE SHEPHERD, WHO DOES NOT OWN THE SHEEP, SEES THE WOLF COMING AND LEAVES THE SHEEP, AND FLEES; AND THE WOLF CATCHES THEM AND SCATTERS THE SHEEP. THE HIRELING FLEES, BECAUSE HE IS A HIRELING, AND CARES NOT FOR THE SHEEP.

I AM THE GOOD SHEPHERD, AND KNOW MY SHEEP, AND THEY KNOW ME.

AND I LAY DOWN MY LIFE FOR THE SHEEP.

AS THE FATHER KNOWS ME, EVEN SO KNOW I THE FATHER.

AND OTHER SHEEP I HAVE, WHICH ARE NOT OF THIS FOLD: THEM ALSO I MUST BRING, AND THEY SHALL HEAR MY VOICE; AND THERE SHALL BE ONE FOLD, AND ONE SHEPHERD.

THEREFORE DOES MY FATHER LOVE ME, BECAUSE I LAY DOWN MY LIFE, THAT I MIGHT TAKE IT AGAIN. NO MAN TAKES IT FROM ME, BUT I LAY IT DOWN, AND I HAVE THE POWER TO TAKE IT AGAIN.

THIS COMMANDMENT HAVE I RECEIVED OF MY FATHER.

121

The NARROW Gate

—ILLUSTRATED BY STEVE CRESPO

"STRIVE TO ENTER IN AT THE STRAIT GATE: FOR MANY, I SAY UNTO YOU, WILL SEEK TO ENTER IN, AND SHALL NOT BE ABLE.

"WHEN ONCE THE MASTER OF THE HOUSE IS RISEN UP, AND HATH **SHUT** TO THE DOOR, AND YE BEGIN TO STAND WITHOUT, AND TO KNOCK AT THE DOOR, SAYING, LORD, LORD, OPEN UNTO US; AND HE SHALL ANSWER AND SAY UNTO YOU, I KNOW YOU **NOT** WHENCE YE ARE:

"THEN SHALL YE BEGIN TO SAY, WE HAVE EATEN AND DRUNK IN THY PRESENCE, AND THOU HAST TAUGHT IN OUR STREETS.

"BUT HE SHALL SAY, I TELL YOU, I KNOW YOU **NOT** WHENCE YE ARE;...

"...DEPART FROM ME, ALL YE WORKERS OF INIQUITY.

LUKE 13:24-30

124

THE END.

These things I have spoken unto you in proverbs: but the time cometh, which I shall no more speak to you in proverbs, but I shall shew you plainly of the Father. At that day ye shall ask in my name: and I say not unto you, that I will pray the Father for you: For the Father himself loveth you, because ye have loved me, and have believed that I came out from God. I came forth from the Father, and am come into the world: again, I leave the world, and go to the Father. His disciples said unto him, Lo, now speakest thou plainly, and speakest no proverb.

John 16:25-29

Mark Ammerman is an illustrator and art director at North Market Street Graphics in Lancaster, Pennsylvania where he lives with his wife, Terri, and their five children. They are members of In The Light Ministries, an interracial, inner-city church. Mark published a comic fanzine, *Comic Courier,* from the mid 60s into the early 70s and contributed art and story to other 'zines in those early years of comic fandom. Currently, Mark and Terri produce the one panel cartoon PreB's for *Celebrate Life,* a national pro-life magazine. Mark is the author of the ongoing historical fiction series "The Cross and the Tomahawk" (Horizon Books).

Rebecca Baerman is a writer, penciller, letterer, and editor, who has worked for several publications. Her interests are comics, learning to ink better, reading, anime, manga and role playing on-line. She would like to eventually have not only her own title, but also her own company.

Leo Bak, adaptor of *Revelation: The Comic Book* lives in Canada with his wife, Lucy Kim. His parents groomed him for medical school, his friends nurtured his stability, but God chose to save him and thrust him into the life of a starving comic book artist.

Michael Bennett is an illustrator living in Ohio with his wife, two daughters, and one dog. When drawing he listens to the 77s, King Crimson and B.B. King. His work has been influenced by Lloyd Ostendorf, Joseph Clement Coll and Jeff Jones. He enjoys the writings of Soren Kierkegaard, Fyodor Dostoevsky, and Robert E. Howard.

Kenn Bivins lives in central Georgia. He is the founder and sole occupant of Somethink Big Studio (unless you count the ant farm, mice, and occasionally misdirected swallows). Kenn has worked with many publishers such as Marvel Comics, and DC Comics.

He is currently preparing his own material for self-publication. Kenn praises God for Jesus (his Lord, Savior, and Friend), for his lovely wife, Angela Rena Bivins, for his son, Kenn II, and the "biscuit in the oven"

Harold Buchholz, creator of *Apathy Kat,* wanted to be a cartoonist from the age of three. He grew up reading a host of classic American comic strips. In college, after reading Robert Short's *The Gospel According To Peanuts*, he realized the powerful impact Christian cartoonists had in introducing him to the faith. Harold and his wife reside in Virginia Beach, Virginia. He offers printing services to short-run and all-ages comic book publishers (including this book).

Danny Bulanadi has worked for DC(i.e., *Legion of Superheroes,* and *Kamandi*) and Marvel Comics(i.e., *Captain America* and *The Fantastic Four*). He also worked for Marvel animation on "The Transformers". In 1986 he became a born again Christian with help from Nestor Redondo. When Marvel filed bankruptcy, his freelance work was not enough to pay the bills. He now works in a different field, waiting for when he might use his talent again....especially for his Lord and Savior, Jesus Christ.

Rick Bundschuh is a writer, cartoonist and the pastor of Kauai Christian Fellowship in Hawaii. He was a regular comic contributor to *Surfer* magazine from 1980 to 1986 and has, over the years, doodled his way into various publications. Rick loves drawing tattoos ... on his four-year-old son... in indelible ink.

Nate Butler has worked as a professional cartoonist and commercial illustrator for over 20 years. He has worked on numerous popular cartoon characters in various media. His studio has packaged several Christian comics including *AidaZee.* Nate is a founder of ROX35 Media, Inc., a nonprofit ministry involved in teaching the production and use of comics for evangelism both here and overseas. Nate was born in 1954, born again in 1979, has a wonderful wife

(Susan), two grown daughters (Carin and Christy), one son-in-law (Scott), and a constant canine companion (Gracie). He lives in Albuquerque, New Mexico.

Sergio Cariello was born in Brazil in 1964 and was born again in 1979 through Brazilian Word of Life Camp, where he came to know Jesus Christ as Lord and Savior. Some of his mainstream credits include the *Deathstroke* monthly series, the *Batman/Wildcat* and the *Catwoman/Wildcat* mini series for DC Comics and *The Avengers* for Marvel Comics. Sergio is an instructor at the Joe Kubert School of Cartoon and Graphic Art. He also leads worship and teaches Sunday school at Redentor Presbyterian Church in South River, New Jersey.

Steve Crespo was born and raised in New York City and is now living in Westchester County, New York with his beautiful wife Eve. Steve has been saved for seven years and making a living in comics for about four (or is it five?) Steve gives thanks for the many lessons the Lord has taught him through the comic book profession. ('specially with *Vampirella* and *Anima*. Ooof!) The hardest lesson has been about faith. Matthew 6:25- 34 has never meant more to him than it does now as a freelancer! Shalom!

Farel Dalrymple was raised by a wonderful Christian woman whom he likes to call "mom". After moving back and forth between Oklahoma and California for 20 years, Farel finally settled in New York. He is currently majoring in illustration at the School of Visual Arts and attends the Village Church in Greenwich.

Greg Dampier is a former police officer turned illustrator, and resides in Daytona Beach, Florida. He has formed a non-profit organization called "Good Fruit Ministry" whose focus is to spread the Gospel to popular culture through comic books.

Jay Disbrow is a comic book artist and writer whose work extends back to the late 1940s and early 1950s. He worked for the famous L.B. Cole and Star Publications. He was also involved in journalism for many years as a feature newspaper and magazine writer. He is the author of the biography "Iger Comics Kingdom."

Newspaper cartoonist/illustrator **Eddie Eddings** fought against God with all his might. His "B.C." years were pocked with sin and grief. He chucked high school to devote himself to music and drugs. Roadblocks, detours, and dead-ends lead him through a hopeless maze into a direct confrontation with Jesus Christ. One night, while alone in his room, he could no longer run. He reached out to the Lord and cried in desperation for salvation. The Lord heard his plea, miraculously and instantly transforming him. Eddie was never the same.

G. Raymond Eddy, a self-taught cartoonist, was born in 1960 and has lived all his life in the farming village of Carrollton, Ohio. His professional projects include *Wild Life* #1 and #2, and *Shanda the Panda* #10 and #12. Cartooning for him is mostly a ministry. The work he is most proud of is his "Galen"strips for K.J. Kolka's *Cardinal Adventures*. The projects he thinks the Lord will most richly reward him for are *Children's Bible Search* and *Proverbs and Parables*. The Word of God is the one thing he can count on to survive the fire at the end of the age and become his reward.

As a child, **Don Ensign** accepted Jesus Christ as his Savior and Lord. He also developed an early interest in comics. He founded the Christian Comic Arts Society (CCAS) in 1984 and the Christian comics APA, *Alpha-Omega*. He works as a graphic artist for a Christian para-church organization in Southern California.

Tim Gagnon was born and raised in Berlin, New Hampshire. With little to no real Christian influence, Tim fell into the trap of the occult at an early age. God rescued him from this and brought him into the service of the Lord Jesus Christ. Tim joined the United States Air Force during the Gulf War and served as a Graphic Specialist designing weapon systems. Later, Tim published a four issue limited series entitled *The Unforgottens*. He is currently working with partner Clint Johnson on a Christian interactive comic titled "Defenders of the Faith". Tim lives in Panama City Beach, Florida with his wife, Christen, and daughter, Lois Sierra.

In accordance with Proverbs 27:2... "What had originally impressed me about Hamm's work in *Scattered* was his attractive artwork. What more impresses me now is his skill at writing a compelling 28 page story" - Jeff Mason, editor of *Indy Magazine*. "...there are genuine glimpses of craft and heart in the [Comics to Bore & Confuse You] tale. Hamm is conducting an interesting experiment, one worth checking out." - cat yronwode in *Comic Buyer' Guide*. This is **Jesse Hamm.**

Steve Firchow was raised in Papua New Guinea by missionary parents and is a science fiction/fantasy illustrator who has worked for Top Cow and is currently the penciler on Liar Comics' *More Than Mortal*.

Michael James started drawing at age 6 and gave his life to Christ at 15. His comic book career began as an inker with Harvey Comics. He has worked for Marvel (*Alf, Heathcliff*), DC Comics (*Tiny Toons*-European market), Disney Afternoon and Harvey's Hanna-Barbera comics. He is currently working on his own projects.

Eric Jensen is an artist and a writer who has self-published *Freedom Fighter* #1 and *Infiltrator* #1 under the imprint of "God and Country Graphics" He has graduated from a three year Bible school, worked as a youth pastor, a singles minister and a teacher in the church on various subjects including, but not limited to, cults and world religions.

Dennis Jensen was truly born in the summer of 1994, when his body had aged forty-two years past the time it first breathed air. Jesus showed him the depth and breath of His grace. The Potter has been continually breaking and remolding that old clay vessel since then. Dennis has inked and penciled numerous comics for both DC Comics (i.e. *Flash, Green Lantern, Blackhawk*); Marvel Comics (i.e. *Marvel Comics Presents, Marvel Super-Heroes*) and for several other publishers.

Clint DeRon Johnson has been a college art teacher and ongoing student. As an avid comic reader he noticed the lack of a positive Christian influence and thus developed Faith Walker, an adventurer combating sin and spiritual ignorance. Faith Walker exemplifies consequential principles outlined in the Bible. Clint is working on the publication of his own comic book.

Hal Jones has been an artist most of his 37 years. Jones lives in St. Clair County, Alabama with his wonderful wife, Kelly, and his two sons, Geoffrey and Stephen. He is a graphic artist, who spends his "spare" time running Soldier Ministries, Inc., an organization dedicated to sharing the Gospel to the world of comics, science-fiction, fantasy and role gaming. He has published *Beyond Human* #0 and *Graven Images Redeemed* #1.

Don Kelly lives in New Bedford, Mass. with his wife and two children. He is a member of *Alpha-Omega* and has recently served as its assistant central mailer. He produces a small press comic strip called "Armadillo Junction".

After college, **Christine Kerrick** worked in a variety of art-related fields. She airbrushed paintings for clients such as Aerosmith, Elton John, former U.S. President George Bush and others. Presently she is creating a series of works based on the book of Revelation. Her book *Empire* was conceived from Christine's personal testimony of the overcoming power of God to conquer pain and to change a human life. She wants to write about how He makes the ugly, broken things in us beautiful.

God touched **K.J. Kolka's** life in two ways at Concordia College, Ann Arbor, Michigan. First, He showed him that faith is not just a Sunday thing, but a lifestyle. Second, He gave Kolka a vision for "The Cardinal," a Christian superhero. Since 1990, The Cardinal has appeared in a free annual tabloid in the Great Lakes area, sponsored by numerous churches and businesses.

Billy Leavell was born in Montgomery, Alabama in 1938, the year of Superman's debut. He loved comics since childhood, devouring newspaper comic strips and then "graduating" to comic books (i.e. Carl Barks' Donald Duck; Superman and Batman). Billy gave his heart to the Lord Jesus at 15 and was immersed into Him. In 1962 he married the former Marilyn Allgood and they have been blessed with three fine children. Being deaf himself, Billy became a minister to the deaf. He uses the comics medium to help his deaf peers understand the Bible, and has published the quarterly periodical *Light for the Deaf* for over 30 years. Billy is one of the founding members of *Alpha-Omega*.

Gary Martin has been inking comics since 1980. He has worked for all the major comic book companies. Gary recently authored the book entitled, "The Art of Comic Book Inking", published in September of 1997 by Dark Horse. Gary currently resides with his wife and daughter in Portland, Oregon and belongs to the Studiosaurus comic art studio. When not inking he spends time with his church's college and career group. For fun he likes to ride his Harley.

Jack Martin is a native Californian, born November 11, 1948. He is a lifelong comics fan, and was involved in the production of *Valiant Efforts*. He loves combining his art with his faith. He hopes you enjoy our efforts.

Mike S. Miller has worked in comics for several years and mostly recently did a five issue, creator-owned series called *The Immortal Two* under the Image Comics imprint. He lives with his wife Meredith in Texas doing video game graphics.

Ralph Ellis Miley received Jesus Christ as Lord and Savior in 1976, while in college. He is married to Desiree, and has three children, Ralph, Janae, and Joy. He has been involved in publishing comics since 1987, having produced *Valiant Efforts* and *The Alpha-Omega Challenge*. Ralph is a member of *Alpha-Omega*, is on the board of the Christian Comic Arts Society, and is the Executive Editor of *New Creation*.

Roman Morales III is an artist and police officer, but

most of all he is a frontline soldier under God's command. Living in Denver, Colorado he is blessed with a beautiful wife, Karen, as well as three wonderfully weird, energetic children; a daughter, Elaina, and twin sons, Aron and Arik.

Bill Morrison comes from the mean streets of Lincoln Park, Michigan. He is Bongo Comics' art director and editor extraordinaire. He received an Eisner Award for his contribution to *Simpsons Comics* #1. He has painted many movie posters for Disney's animated films, including "The Little Mermaid," "Bambi," and "Peter Pan." He also fulfilled a life-long dream by contributing to Dark Horse Comics' line of *Tex Avery* titles.

Win Mumma can best be described as a commercial artist who would rather be a cartoonist. For a number of years he wrote and drew the "O.T." (for Old Testament) cartoon series for *TQ* magazine, a youth publication put out by Back to the Bible Broadcast. A number of these strips were later reformatted into four "Cosmics" comic books published by Tyndale House Publishers. He is now self-employed as an illustrator, designer and, as often as possible, a cartoonist.

David Murphy was born in Montana. He and his wife now reside in the Seattle, Wa. area. Their daughter, Melissa, was his assistant on this project. His inspiration came from a desire to portray Jesus as a Shepherd who fights for his flock, sometimes violently.

Devin Parker lives in the mountains of southern California. He is an art student and a member of *Alpha-Omega* specializing in manga-style comic strips.

Jim Pinkoski is a 7th-day Adventist Christian who wanted to be a cartoonist since he was 10. He grew up in California and now lives in Tennessee. In 1976 he worked in Neal Adams' Continuity Studio, and in 1988

did cartoons for Carl Sagan. In 1989 he met Ron Wyatt, an archeologist who has a museum near Nashville which Jim managed for 2 1/2 years. Jim and his wife Sandra have been involved with the Gatlinburg/Smoky Mountain Passion Play. Jim currently has 5 books in print with 1/4 million sold, available from Amazing Facts.

Drew Pocza lives near the ski resort of Big Bear Lake in southern California. Drew is in his late twenties and was born again in 1989. His favorite book of the Bible is Philippians.

Mark Poe was born November 1961 on Sand Mountain in North Alabama. Several things have been pivotal in his life. He accepted Jesus Christ as Savior at the age of twelve. Mark met Rhonda Biddle in the llth grade and promptly asked her to marry him. Their son, Brian Scott, was born in 1987. Mark joined the *Alpha-Omega* APA in 1985, where he met Freazie White Jr. and published *Project: New Man* in 1991. He met Todd Tennant in 1997 and formed Mega Comics.

J.D. Ray was born and raised in central Illinois and had a natural talent for art. He now works as an independent colorist of Heroic Age Studios. He has worked on DC comic book covers and interior art. His credits also include a number of *Sonic the Hedgehog* and other Sega related comic book covers for Archie Comics.

Bud Rogers, a self taught artist and cartoonist, has contributed numerous comic strips and cartoons to the *Comic Buyer's Guide*. His character "Awesomedude" has appeared in *CBG, The Alpha-Omega Challenge* and *New Creation*. Bud is currently concentrating on several projects geared toward preschoolers.

Gary Shipman and his wife Rhoda are the creators of Caliber Comic's acclaimed fantasy series, *Pakkins' Land*. They and their baby daughter live in northern California.

Howard Simpson was born and raised in Newark, New Jersey. He began drawing storyboards for "Action-News" and "Accu-Weather" while attending Temple University's Tyler School of Art. He has done freelance work for publishers such as Marvel Comics, DC Comics,

Dark Horse and Acclaim. His current projects include "Zone 26," and "The Never Ending Jam" plus development of various CD-ROMs and web-sites.

Alec Stevens was born in 1965 in Salvador, Brazil and was reared in a Christian family. However it was not until late 1989 that Alec dedicated his life to Jesus Christ after years of selfish pursuits and prodigal living. Professionally, his illustrations have appeared in the *New York Times Book Review,* and *The New Yorker*. His comic book career includes two graphic novels for DC/Piranha Press, and work for many other publishers. He is an instructor at the Joe Kubert School of Cartoon and Graphic Art, and is presently recording a twelve song CD of his own music to accompany a graphic novel.

Geoff Strout is a San Diego-based student and graphic artist. He has had experience illustrating various projects. As God's word, the Bible is the one truly valuable message we have to communicate. Because of this Geoff has often entertained the notion of doing a Biblically based project, but has never done any work towards that end until now.

Andre Szymanowicz was born and raised in southeast Pennsylvania. He received salvation at the early age of 5. He was a recent student at the Joe Kubert School of Cartoon and Graphic Arts. He has since abandoned the safety of school and moved on to pursue his dream of freelancing and self-publishing. His favorite verse of Scripture is II Peter 3:9.

In his pre-Christian days, **Todd Tennant** was a rock drummer. God took him out of that lifestyle and blessed him suddenly with the ability to draw. Todd and his wife Tina lives in the Guntersville, Alabama area with three children, where he works as an architectural artist. Todd has also worked for such Christian publishers as Moody Monthly and David C. Cook Publishing. With writer Mike Sares, he has published a comic book called *Private Sector*.

Kyle Vannoy sensed God's presence in his life ever since he was very young. He is still trying to decipher his calling and glorify God through any talent he may have.

Bill Webb was born in California at Edwards Air Force Base in 1957. Bill was an avid comic reader, enjoying the art of such legends as Jack Kirby, Steve Ditko, Carmine Infantino and Nick Cardy. He also was a fan of animation, relishing the work of the Hanna-Barbara studios. In 1980, he moved to Washington state to be closer to his future wife, Kathleen, whom he married in 1981. He works at the *Tacoma News Tribune* in the Graphic Arts Department, has written stories for Archie Comics and done freelance work for Gospel Light. He accepted the Lord in 1979, and attends a Baptist

General Conference church with his wife. They live near the city of Tacoma.

Kathleen Webb was born in Puyallup, Washington in 1956. She accepted her Savior and Lord, Jesus Christ, when she was only four. She was raised in a godly home, for which she is thankful. At age ten she discovered the legendary Archie artist Dan DeCarlo. After managing to survive a brief flirtation with the bulging biceps of superhero art, she settled into her own style. In 1985 she landed a job at Archie Comics writing and penciling. She produces a one page color comic, "Holly and the Ivy Halls", for Focus on the Family's *BRIO* magazine, and has done work of Gospel Light. Kathleen and Bill live with their three cats, Noelle, Velvet, and Mink. As far as being a Proverbs 31 woman, after thirty-six years, she says she's still workin' at it.

Edgar J. Williams is an artist and writer whose chief goal is to glorify God with the talents that He has given him, and to use those talents to lead others to a saving faith in Jesus Christ. Originally from Milwaukee, Wis., he now makes his home in Atlanta, Ga. with his beautiful wife Maeryia and their three children; Keshonda, David, and Danielle. When he isn't drawing bridges for the state of Ga., or teaching Sunday school, He designs Christian t-shirts, draws comics, writes, and teaches "How to Draw Comic Heroes God's Way", a class he developed that teaches young aspiring artists how to draw comic characters from a Christian perspective.

Monte Wilson has been drawing comic books for six years and is currently a member of Alpha-Omega. He is the writer/artist of the independently published *Royal Guard* and *elfin Romance* and he has been known to sing "Oklahoma" at the drop of a hat..

By day, **Chris Yambar** works as an internationally recognized pop artist. By night, Chris works as a professional cartoonist, writer and comic book publisher. His best known character, Mr. Beat, is quickly becoming a cult mainstay in the industry. Chris explains that the most important event in his life had little to do with his career. It was making an intelligent and sober decision to accept the gift of salvation through the sacrifice of Jesus Christ. "I didn't decide to follow Jesus to get out of Hell or get an afterlife insurance policy. I decided to follow Him because He made complete sense and didn't insult my intelligence."

Kevin Yong was born and raised in southern California. Kevin was "home schooled" through high school and then took two years off to study Christian apologetics before beginning his "normal" college education. When not busy with his studies, Kevin works as a writer/editor on the *New Creation* newsletter and is a prolific participant in the *Alpha-Omega* apazine.

And also...

Carlos Garzon was born in Bogota, Colombia in 1945. He currently lives in New York and has worked for DC Comics (i.e. *Batman, Legion of Super-Heroes, Hawkman*), Marvel Comics (i.e. *Spider-Man, Incredible Hulk, Ka-Zar*) and on various licensed characters (i.e. *Star Wars, Star Trek, Flash Gordon, Bugs Bunny, Bullwinkle and Rocky*). He also serves as an instructor for ROX 35 Media, Inc.'s Christian Comics Training Course.

Gene Yang lives in northern California. He is the creator of *Gordon Yamamoto and the King of the Geeks*, a winner of the Xeric Grant.

Randy Emberlin is an Oregon-based inker who has worked on numerous comic book series for Marvel Comics and Dark Horse Comics.